Adventures in Eden

AN INTIMATE TOUR OF THE PRIVATE GARDENS OF EUROPE

Carolyn Mullet

TIMBER PRESS • PORTLAND, OREGON

Published in 2020 by Timber Press, Inc.

The Haseltine Building
133 S.W. Second Avenue, Suite 450
Portland, Oregon 97204-3527
timberpress.com

Printed in China

Text design by Hillary Caudle
Jacket design by Rita Sowins

ISBN 978-1-60469-846-6

Catalog records for this book are available from the Library of Congress and the British Library.

Contents

Introduction

THE PRIVATE GARDEN has a special place in the roster of outdoor spaces. At its core, it is deeply intertwined with the emotional idea of home, that most intimate place where we live our daily lives and the place we return to over and over again for comfort and safety. Just like the inside of our houses, our gardens are places where we express our personal identity but with the added challenge that the expression must be made in collaboration with nature, that great teacher of humility and patience. The rewards for the devoted garden owner are moments of sheer beauty that most interior spaces have a hard time matching.

This book celebrates the private garden by exploring the stories behind fifty gardens scattered across Europe. I have heard that we are living in a golden age of garden making. Time will tell if that is so, but we are certainly in an era when noteworthy gardens are being created and parts of older gardens are being revamped to make them more of our time. This book is a snapshot of that burst of activity in European private gardens over the last twenty-five years, with one added factor: the owners of these gardens open their gates to the public at some time each year and we are welcomed in.

I came to my enthusiasm for private gardens during a thirty-year career as a garden designer in the Washington, D.C., area. When social media made it easier to become familiar with gardens around the globe, I discovered that the kinds of gardens I liked, others liked also, and to my amazement, my followers grew to more than a million on Facebook and more than 40,000 on Instagram. Because I believe that gardens are cultural expressions worthy of attention just like painting, sculpture, theater, and music, I started Carex Tours, a niche garden-tour company, to enable others to visit gardens in person to explore how someone else makes a garden space, arranges plants, provides resting places, or connects their garden to their surroundings. My wish for my travelers is that the atmosphere and beauty of the gardens will be in some way inspiring.

I hope that readers will see the book as a somewhat idiosyncratic overview of the state of private garden design in Europe in the early twenty-first century, where size or status has had nothing to do with the choices, but passion, plantsmanship, and creativity has meant everything.

Engla

nd

Broughton Grange

BANBURY, OXFORDSHIRE

IN THE ROLLING COUNTRYSIDE of Oxfordshire in South East England is a new walled garden that boldly defies the idea that has dominated English gardens for the last one hundred years: the hedged garden room. Designed by Tom Stuart-Smith, the one-and-a-half-acre garden at Broughton Grange has a singular sweeping panorama with few structural elements to interrupt the view. "I like everything to be interconnected," he explains, "one overall story, with a series of subplots, not a series of episodes. I want the whole garden to be one malleable entity" (Richardson 2013).

The gardens at Broughton Grange dated from the Victorian era until the current owner, Stephen Hester, asked Tom in 2000 to design a contemporary garden. Stephen was inspired by the open parterres of the gardens at Château de Villandry and by a novel he had read as a child—*The Secret Garden*, written in 1911 by Frances Hodgson Burnett. In a break with convention, they chose a site that was not connected to the house. In a sloping paddock some distance away, Tom created a destination garden, enclosed on the west and north sides by handsome brick walls. The space opens to the sunnier sides, with views of the surrounding bucolic valley. Within the walls, Tom divided the garden into three spacious terraces, each with its own atmosphere and planting style.

On the lowest level is a parterre of velvety, rounded boxwood in what appears to be an abstract pattern; it is, however, based on an enlargement of the microscopic cellular structure of leaves in the hedgerows outside the garden. Seasonal plantings fill the spaces between the parterre "venation," with a particularly effective display of jewel-toned tulips in spring. On either side of the parterre are paths edged in borders overflowing with nepeta, alchemilla, hardy geranium, astrantia, and phlox. As one walks through this garden, it is easy to admire Tom's skill in creating an artful, modern interpretation of a traditional garden form.

From the parterre terrace, one ascends perfectly proportioned steps to the middle level. At the center is a rectangular pond, with thick stepping stones floating just above the waterline. On this terrace, one can pause at a stone sitting area. The openness draws the attention across the water to the gentle, rural vista. On either side of the pond, Tom shows his preference for contemporary, naturalistic plantings accented with topiary. Masses of *Rodgersia pinnata*, *Persicaria polymorpha*, and *Calamagrostis ×acutiflora* 'Overdam' spill onto the single path, while shaped beech stand like pawns on a chessboard.

A final set of steps leads to the deep, upper terrace covered in a veritable sea of lemon-, lavender-, rose-, and pearl-colored plants. On this level, Tom created a ravishing plant tapestry punctuated with thin, dark yew columns. It seems impenetrable, but on closer inspection, one discovers narrow one-person paths. Eryngium, phlomis, stachys, and stipa grasses arch over these paths, reminding the visitor to look down and step around a mound of lamb's ears or a cluster of allium. Eventually, one comes to a rill that flows into the pond below, a place of calm in an otherwise intense and near-wild space. From here, the contrasting soft hills, fields, and hedgerows of the surrounding landscape are impossible to miss.

Although the rill, as the garden's water source, seems like the heart of the garden, Stephen notes that, for him, in a counterintuitive way, the heart is the surrounding beautiful English valley. The garden feels at one with the countryside, and yet it is set apart.

With the Walled Garden, Tom brought twenty-first-century design to Broughton Grange. Stephen has other projects in mind. In addition to the Walled Garden are a new eighty-acre arboretum, fifty acres of parkland, and twenty-five acres of other gardens and lightly cultivated woodlands—plenty of space for more experiments and changes. Is it any wonder that being in this special place gives him a palpable feeling of beauty and tranquility whenever he arrives?

OPPOSITE Sumptuous perennials, trees, and shrubs line the main path that connects the three terraces.

On the upper terrace, plants are trained vertically on
a brick wall, while a rich planting of perennials and
grasses creates textural and color interest in the beds
surrounding a path.

FROM TOP A rill slices through the dense planting on the upper terrace. • A narrow gravel path, surrounded by salvias, geraniums, lamb's ears, and alliums, leads to a stepping stone placed in the middle of the rill.

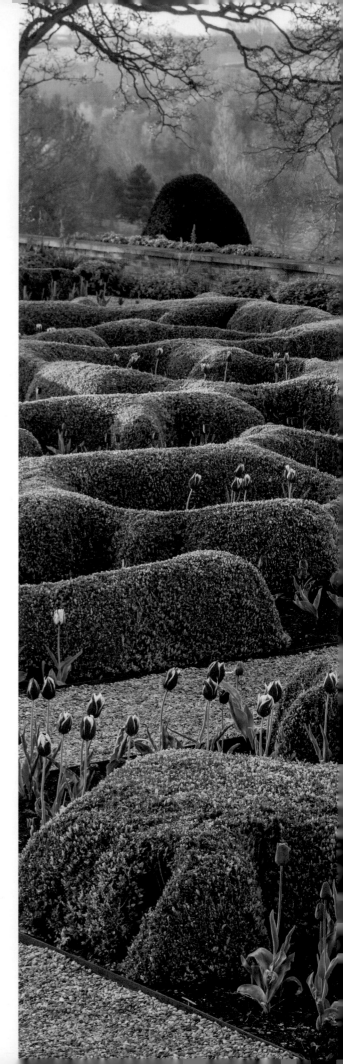

FROM TOP The large pond and patio are the focus of the middle terrace, open spaces that afford views across the garden to the countryside beyond. • An open gate flanked by massed hostas offers a glimpse into the colorful garden.

RIGHT In spring, the lower terrace parterre is dotted with jewel-toned tulips.

Bryan's Ground

STAPLETON, HEREFORDSHIRE

IN RURAL HEREFORDSHIRE, along the sinuous River Lugg that separates England from Wales, is Bryan's Ground, a formal garden with a generous dash of contemporary wildness. Owners David Wheeler and Simon Dorrell made their initial decisions about the garden soon after they moved there in November 1993, when they confidently drew outlines of a design in newly fallen snow.

The property included a handsome 1913 house. It was built in the local half-timbered style, typical of the era's influential Arts and Crafts movement, in which handcraftsmanship was preferred over mass production and gardens harmonized with their houses and the surrounding countryside. These ideas have held sway over David and Simon as well.

The couple's first venture in making the garden was in an area next to the driveway entrance. Seeing some depressions in the soil, they deduced that at one time this had been an orchard, and they immediately decided to plant thirty heritage apple trees of different varieties, arranged in a grid. Each tree was placed in the middle of a ten-foot square, underplanted with *Iris sibirica* 'Papillon', which flowers in soft lavender-blue from May to early June. In February, when the points of the iris leaves are just about to peep from the soil, they are covered in a blue haze of *Anemone blanda*. David and Simon blithely refer to this successful succession as high tide and low tide.

A decade later, they added a shallow canal through the orchard, its brick edges emphasizing the view to the house from the driveway, augmenting the visitor's arrival experience with a year-round feature.

If it seems that the pair is particularly at ease with garden design, one can look to their professional lives for the explanation. David is the publisher and editor of the literary gardening quarterly *Hortus* (which *Gardinista* called "the *New Yorker* of horticultural reading" [Wilson 2017]), and Simon is its art editor, who also paints landscapes and designs gardens.

It was Simon who conceived the garden's structure. As a devotee of Arts and Crafts architecture, he believes that the role of a garden is to be an intermediary between the house and the extended landscape. "The position of every design element is dictated by the design of the house in terms of layout, scale, and proportion," he explains, "and relates directly to landmarks beyond the garden boundary, be it a tree, a hill, or a distant church."

From remnants of an earlier garden close to the house, David and Simon fashioned hedged rooms with topiaries, parterres, fountains, and reflecting pools. The existing kitchen garden and greenhouse were updated. Follies were built of locally grown oak, larch, and Douglas fir. Paths were created of nearby quarried stone and gravel, and borders include colorful perennials—some bold, others wispy. On the kitchen garden wall hangs a piece of slate inscribed with a quote from Shakespeare's *Twelfth Night*: "In delay there lies no plenty."

Fanning out beyond these formal gardens, David planted a collection of 240 *Hydrangea* species and an arboretum crisscrossed with straight, mown paths. The arboretum has grown to include more than 1000 trees spread over five acres. In spring, the air is filled with the sweet fragrance of *Rhododendron luteum* and the ground glows with thousands of blooming bulbs.

Despite all this serious effort to bring order to Bryan's Ground, the rules of formal gardening are not slavishly followed. Self-seeders are allowed to proliferate. Weeds beneficial to wildlife are welcomed. Shrubs heavy with blossoms bend deeply into pathways. Roses tumble over campanulas. Teasels invade lavender and foxgloves. Aquilegia seedlings sprout so thickly that they become groundcovers.

One wonders if this insouciant dishevelment is the result of Simon's childhood experience of playing in a derelict garden designed by Gertrude Jekyll. Or perhaps the couple has taken to heart, more deeply than most English garden makers, the dictum first pronounced by Vita Sackville-West, that a successful garden must have "the strictest formality of design, with the maximum informality in planting."

Over the years as the gardens were being made and the outbuildings cleaned up, the couple has unearthed bits and pieces from the everyday lives of former inhabitants of Bryan's Ground. Both men feel attached to these mini-archeological finds and display them in clever ways throughout the garden. Rusty bicycles and old shoes hang from trees. Grasses grow through a curving bed frame. A classical bust of a pretty woman sports a rusty chain around her neck. Porcelain fragments are individually displayed in the small compartments of a wooden printer's tray. There's a sense of artful fun in this garden, a place for nature, passion, and serendipity.

Enveloped in wildness, a simple wooden cabin built by Simon flanks the
edge of the stream-fed Strongacre Pool next to the River Lugg.

ABOVE Wisteria heavy with fragrant racemes adorns the loggia, its color creating the perfect complement to the ochre-colored dovecote at the end of the path.

LEFT The perimeter of Bryan's Ground has *claire-voies*, light-filled openings, where the garden and the greater landscape intermingle.

Near the house is the George Walk, named after the couple's first Labrador Retriever, with a formal pool shaped like a geometric dog bone and a handsome dog sculpture.

RIGHT A shallow border featuring soft fennel, *Anchusa azurea* 'Loddon Royalist', and *Stachys byzantina* extends along the back of the house, with an eccentrically shaped hedge demonstrating David and Simon's playful style.

Cothay Manor and Gardens

GREENHAM, SOMERSET

TO VISIT COTHAY MANOR, located in the deepest southern part of Somerset, one must drive along sunken country lanes covered with overgrown hedgerow plants that softly whoosh above. "Cothay is set near nowhere," says Mary-Anne Robb, the owner and creative force behind the manor's gardens. On arrival, visitors may feel as though they have discovered a secret garden, albeit one that happens to surrounds a 500-year-old moated house that is frequently hailed as the finest small medieval manor in England. No wonder many call it a magical place.

It was not always so. When Mary-Anne and her late husband came to Cothay Manor in 1995 and began serious restoration, very little remained of the garden created in the 1920s by Colonel Reginald Cooper except for its structure: yew hedges delineating garden rooms. He was, of course, following the dominant and most fashionable idea in that era's gardens when he wrapped the garden around the manor house and organized his rooms along a 200-yard yew-hedged walk.

Mary-Anne decided to leave the hedge framework, saying now that it was the best decision she made in those early years, and began gutting each of the garden rooms. Today the themed rooms are planted with her signature soft-toned color schemes. Emily's Garden, named for her first granddaughter, is filled with yellow and cream-colored plants. The Bishop's Garden is inspired by Mary-Anne's favorite uncle, with blossoms of episcopal reds and purples. The Green Knight Garden is planted in only white flowers. In each room are first-rate, old stone objects. "I'm not particular," she says, "but I do like the best!"

One of the simplest and most serene garden rooms is the Walk of the Unicorn—a long, narrow avenue lined on both sides with forty *Robinia pseudoacacia* 'Umbraculifera'. A stone-edged gravel path crosses at the center, with a particularly fine, stone unicorn in the middle. In the spring, thousands of white tulips (*Tulipa* 'White Triumphator') bloom gracefully under the trees, giving way in early summer to the exuberant violet-blue wildness of *Nepeta* 'Six Hills Giant'. The effect is elegant and dreamy.

Summer is Mary-Anne's favorite time in the gardens. Annual sweet peas in ravishing colors, sown the year before, scramble and climb everywhere. Ten large terracotta pots filled with half-hardy perennials are at their frothy best. Show-stopping acanthus display their statuesque flower spikes that tower above handsome, shiny leaves. A spectacular *Catalpa bignonioides* produces many clusters of white blossoms flecked in purple and yellow. "The garden looks like a fairyland," she says with justified pride.

Walking through the gardens, one soon appreciates the confident artistic vision at work. Mary-Anne says that structure and repeated plantings are the most important elements that hold her gardens together. But she is also quite comfortable with wildness and has ceded some control to nature. Self-seeders run wild on the main stone terrace next to the house, filling every joint and crevice. Moving up and down steps involves threading one's way around flowery trespassers. Walls and benches are enveloped by wandering plants. Fences in the surrounding park have been torn down to add a wildflower meadow, abuzz with pollinators. While strolling along the River Tone that runs through the garden, one sees a wispy, rambling naturalism everywhere.

Terracotta planters in the lawn overflow with annuals and half-hardy perennials, including *Argyranthemum* 'Mary Wootton', *Salvia fulgens*, *Diascia barberae*, and sweet peas.

OPPOSITE An open Gothic wooden gate offers an enticing glimpse of the medieval manor house and entry garden.

Some plants, such as *Alchemilla mollis*, are allowed to seed wantonly into
cracks and crannies in the gardens' stone steps and walls.

Along the path through the Walk of the Unicorn is *Robinia pseudoacacia* 'Umbraculifera', underplanted with *Nepeta* 'Six Hills Giant'.

A central path leads through a double border blooming with *Alchemilla mollis*, *Verbascum chaixii* 'Album', and alstroemeria.

Fairlight End

PETT, EAST SUSSEX

CHRIS AND ROBIN HUTT'S eighteenth-century house at Fairlight End is perched on a high ridge overlooking the Sussex Weald, one of forty-six designated Areas of Outstanding Natural Beauty in the United Kingdom. The weald is an ancient landscape of steeply sloped hills, dense woodlands, and hummocky hedgerows. The scenic view influenced much of the development of the three-acre garden's outward-looking design.

The couple moved to the property in 2004, knowing that they preferred a twenty-first-century garden in outlook and materials. "We wanted to make a garden of our time," explains Robin, a photographer with training in fine art, rather than one that "hark[s] back to an earlier age." The Hutts' plan was to develop the land naturalistically with wildflower meadows and ponds. Inspiration for this approach came from a visit Chris made in the 1980s to Ashton Wold, the home and garden of Dame Miriam Rothschild, the great naturalist and entomologist. "The house was grand," he says, "but the garden was completely wild and full of butterflies. It was like nowhere I had previously visited. I was captivated and never forgot Ashton Wold."

The same year the Hutts moved to Fairlight End, Christopher Lloyd, the erudite owner of Great Dixter, published his book *Meadows*. Lloyd's world-famous garden was a mere twelve miles away, so when Great Dixter offered a course on meadow-making, Chris attended not once but twice. He says now, "The serendipity of living close by a world expert publishing a key work was so helpful in getting us off to a good start with our own meadows."

Within a few years, ponds were dug and the meadow areas sown by hand using seed collected from old farms by a local conservation organization. Two years later, the Hutts augmented the original sowing with freshly cut material from the established meadows at Great Dixter. Now, oxeye daisy and common spotted orchid mingle with yellow rattle, betony, and red campion peaking in mid-June. The meadow "is breathtaking to sit in, lie in, or just walk through, particularly early in the morning, or towards sundown," says Chris. The key to their success, he believes, is not to cut the meadow too early, so that the seeds it contains have time to set and then drop.

The Hutts asked Ian Kitson, a landscape architect and garden designer known for his sinuous designs, to create level living areas closer to the house. He terraced the slope, using a thin, curvaceous band of Corten steel as a retaining wall. Above the wall and close to the house is a swath of lawn, and below, an intimate, serpentine deck offers a quiet place to enjoy the view. Though it was a simple solution, its effect is dramatic, and it injects a distinctly modern note in an otherwise naturalistic garden.

It has not escaped the Hutts' attention that many wild gardens can appear quite disheveled outside the growing season. To create an attractive year-round garden, they have balanced the wildness with a kind of abstract topiary. "This sounds formal," says Chris, "but it isn't the way we do it. We only clip curving, rounded, sinuous, asymmetric shapes. And we clip native deciduous species such as hawthorn, hornbeam, beech, as much as we do evergreens," including yew, holly, dwarf mountain pines, and pittosporum.

The development of this modern, scenic garden has required commitment and persistence from the Hutts and a willingness to ask for help when necessary. With the successes they've experienced so far, they are prepared to nurture Fairlight End to maturity. "We are now encouraging the wildness to invade the garden nearer to the windows of our home," says Chris. "Where will we stop? Who knows?"

Stepping stones lead through an appealing planting of *Verbascum chaixii* 'Album', *Stachys officinalis* 'Hummelo', *Stipa gigantea*, *Nepeta* 'Leeds Castle', and clipped box balls.

OPPOSITE A view over the winter garden from the second floor of the house highlights the Hutts' topiary collection and the pastoral view beyond.

A thin Corten steel retaining wall separates the manicured lawn from the wildflower meadow and provides a nook for an intimate deck with views to the Sussex Weald.

Hanham Court Gardens

HANHAM ABBOTS, SOUTH GLOUCESTERSHIRE

LOCATED IN THE COUNTRYSIDE between Bristol and Bath in Somerset, Hanham Court is a former monastery with a church and tythe barn dating from the Middle Ages. Although there were architectural additions and augmentations during the Tudor, Gothic, Georgian, and Arts and Crafts periods, the gardens were another story. When renowned garden designers Julian and Isabel Bannerman purchased the property in 1993, the place was dilapidated, and, other than a lawn, the grounds were overgrown with a tangle of brambles and brooding Leyland cypress trees. But by 2010, *Gardens Illustrated*, the English magazine that for many is the arbiter of the best and the brightest in garden design, declared Hanham Court to be the "No. 1 Dreamy Garden."

The Bannermans came to Hanham Court's twenty-five acres with a well-developed vision of the kind of garden they wanted. They are known for creating romantic gardens filled with artful, historical references and lavish, fragrant plantings, and restoring a medieval ruin seemed an inevitable next step. The transformation took twenty years, and then the Bannermans moved on. Since 2015, Richard and Julia Boissevain have made Hanham Court their home and are restoring the gardens to the glory of the Bannermans' tenure.

To visit the gardens, one steps through a large, Tudor-style gateway into a dim, cool, stone-walled room. Ahead, a wide stone arch topped with dangling wisteria blooms frames a view of sky, distant rolling hills, and a long, narrow bowling green lawn. Along the gravel paths that border the lawn, tall yew topiaries march in a rhythmic line toward the horizon, their shapes reminiscent of slenderized chess queens, with topknots where their crowns would be.

Behind the topiaries are a series of beds overflowing with dozens and dozens of old roses. Their blossom-laden branches tumble over one another, scrambling up Gothic archways and toppling into paths. Spires of delphiniums and blowsy peony blossoms share space with regal lilies and brilliantly colored lupines. In the middle of the plantings is a swimming pool, shrouded in fragrant shrubs and roses and hidden behind stone walls built as ruins around repurposed Gothic windows and heavily pedimented stone columns.

Close by is a timber gateway to another space. Its exaggerated cornices suggest the designer was having a bit of neoclassical fun. The gravel space is bordered in large obelisks and balustrades. Water trickles from three ox heads into a large, stone water trough set against the glossy leaves of espaliered *Magnolia grandiflora*. White roses abound in fragrant, floral columns.

Reaching the outer edges of these captivating plantings, one realizes that this part of the garden is on a high retaining wall with broad views to the surrounding landscape. On the hillside is an apple and pear orchard. A meadow, filled with poppies, cornflowers, and daisies, blends into a rough pasture that spreads across the rest of the undulating land. Mown paths wind to the top of the slope, and from there, one can see how the ancient retaining walls project into the landscape, a romantic and floriferous peninsula jutting into the gentle terrain.

Fragrant *Rosa* 'Félicité Perpétue' blooms lean into a pathway in early summer.

OPPOSITE Wisteria is skillfully trained over the back of the house.

A repurposed Gothic stone window embellishes one end of
the swimming pool garden.

An elegant stone
archway frames the
view of yew topiary.

Along a gravel path, iris
and euphorbia lighten
the solidity of clipped
boxwood balls.

Hillside

NEAR BATH, SOMERSET

AS ONE OF BRITAIN'S most respected garden and landscape designers, Dan Pearson is known for his sensitive approach to place and his deep horticultural knowledge. He and his partner, Huw Morgan, lived in London until 2010, with the constraints of an overflowing city garden. The longing for a broader horizon came to the fore when the couple visited friends in the idyllic, rolling farmland north of Bath in Somerset. "I wanted to be part of something bigger; somewhere it was possible to let the eye travel and to garden with blurred boundaries," Dan wrote in *Dig Delve*, his weekly online magazine. "I wanted to be part of a place, a smaller cog in a bigger cycle; one that I might learn to steer rather than have to control in entirety."

Dan and Huw purchased a farmstead on top of a steep, south-facing hillside with beautiful views across a valley to the crest of the hills beyond. Stretching along a contour line near the top of the twenty acres are the house and assorted outbuildings. The southern boundary of the land is formed by a stream at the bottom of a slope, and on the rest of the property, farm fields are rich with fertile soil.

As one would expect, the pair approached the site with careful attention to its sense of place and context. The hard landscaping and architectural interventions that they built referred to the agricultural aesthetic of the old farmstead. The plantings were informed by Dan's close observation of natural plant communities, such as wetlands and meadows. He worked with native flora to enhance biodiversity, while using these communities as inspiration for the ornamental plantings in the garden. His intention was "to create a seamless link between the native flora of the surrounding managed landscape and the horticulture of the ornamental gardens," he says, to create "a place that feels without boundaries and is connected to its surroundings."

After a few years, they built retaining walls to level the areas around the buildings so that gardening would be easier. On the plateau next to the house is the Herb Garden, which is not planted with kitchen herbs but with a range of dry-climate and Mediterranean plants, including lavender, *Opopanax chironium*, giant fennel, flax, salvia, and calamint—fragrant pollinator plants in shades of blues and mauves enlivened with acid yellows, white, and bright pinks.

The gateway to the Kitchen Garden is surrounded by two massive, eighteenth-century granite troughs filled with water. Sixteen raised beds edged in rusted steel are planted with a wide selection of vegetables, including artichokes, asparagus, potatoes, and climbing beans, as well as a selection of soft fruits, such as raspberries, gooseberries, loganberries, blackcurrants, and a Japanese wineberry. Espaliered pears and cherries are trained on the rear retaining wall, and pumpkins grow in the compost heaps beyond the barns and in a circular raised bed edged with stone.

In front of the house and down the slope is the Milking Barn, which has been converted into a home office. On one side is a courtyard, separated by a ha-ha (a ditch with a retaining wall on its inner side that keeps animals at bay while providing uninterrupted views). Another granite trough anchors the space, surrounded by a stand of giant fennel and a groundcover planting in shades of yellow and magenta, with *Sanguisorba officinalis* 'Tanna', *Achillea* 'Moonshine', *Geranium sanguineum* 'Tiny Monster', *Euphorbia ceratocarpa*, and *Dianthus carthusianorum*.

On the other side of the Milking Barn is the Perennial Garden that slopes down to the fields. Planted naturalistically to sit well into the surrounding landscape, fine-textured plant combinations are color themed with eye-catching reds, yellows, and oranges closer to the building, and more recessive pinks, mauves, blues, and white toward the garden boundaries. Dan has paid special attention to the scale and color of the surrounding fields and native vegetation, adding a large number of sanguisorbas, ornamental forms of the native grass *Deschampsia cespitosa*, and the giant thornless thistle, *Cirsium canum*.

When asked what they love most about their garden, Huw supplied the answer: "It provides everything we need—a connection to nature, views, beauty, food, comfort, activity, work, play, thought, and contemplation."

OPPOSITE Planted along the gravel path in the Perennial Garden are *Sanguisorba* 'Tanna', *Knautia macedonica*, *Salvia nemorosa* 'Amethyst', *Thalictrum* 'Elin', and *Calamintha sylvatica* 'Menthe'.

Sheep graze in the pastures beyond plantings of *Sanguisorba* 'Red Thunder',
Chamaenerion angustifolium 'Album', and *Thalictrum* 'White Splendide'.

HILLSIDE

In the Kitchen Garden, a wide selection of vegetables fill
sixteen beds edged in rusted steel.

The views from the Milking Barn studio below the house
include the sweeping hillsides and the Perennial Garden,
where *Lilium pardalinum*, *Dierama pulcherrimum*
'Guinevere', *Euphorbia wallichii*, and *Geranium* 'Patricia'
are planted.

Norney Wood

SHACKLEFORD, SURREY

NORNEY WOOD is Jean and Richard Thompson's ten-acre property in the scenic Surrey Hills near the village of Shackleford, an hour west of London. In 2006, when the couple moved into the hundred-year-old house, the property had no garden. "On the positive side," says Richard, "we did inherit a mature collection of oak, beech, pine, larch, and holly and a glorious bank of rhododendron, which all serve to make a wonderful backdrop."

This part of Surrey was the domain of gardening grand dame Gertrude Jekyll in the late nineteenth and early twentieth centuries, and she made her home at Munstead Wood, just a few miles away from Norney Wood. When they created their garden wish list, the Thompsons opted for "Gertrude Jekyll with a modern twist." They admired her use of hardscaping with local materials and strong perpendicular lines and her plantings of hedges, traditional roses, and perennials in drifts. Enlisting the help of Debbie Roberts and Ian Smith of Acres Wild, a landscape architecture firm in West Sussex, they drew up a garden plan, and construction began in 2008.

Because the Thompsons are devoted gardeners who are keenly aware of the natural world, it was important to them that their new home and garden look not only to the past for design inspiration but also look forward to address the environmental issues of the twenty-first century. Before walls, ponds, and flower borders were constructed, about 8000 feet of trenches were excavated to accommodate the ground-source heat collectors for their home's heating system. In addition, two 1850-gallon cisterns were buried in the front of the house to store roof rainwater for use in the garden, and a borehole was sunk in the woods to top up the cisterns automatically in dry periods. What would have been a difficult retrofit in an established garden was easily accommodated before the first stone was laid. Starting a garden from scratch can have its advantages.

Visitors enter the garden through the West Courtyard, marked by four *Malus* 'Evereste' trees, and step into the Reception Garden, a welcoming space with a tiered fountain. Beyond is the main terrace, with a pleached lime walk—an allée of tilia sheared into a narrow aerial hedge—that forms a green architectural edge to the formal, rectangular lawn. A dining terrace paved in recycled Yorkstone spans the back of the house, along with plantings of fragrant *Rosa* 'Gertrude Jekyll' (appropriate) and *Lavandula angustifolia* 'Hidcote'.

A broad stone walk that borders the other side of the lawn is swathed in billowy *Nepeta racemosa* 'Walker's Low', *Stachys byzantina* 'Silver Carpet', and *Rosa* 'The Generous Gardener'. At the end of the walk is a small stucco-and-stone building with a wide, arched entrance. The Thompsons call it the Thunder House: according to Richard, Jekyll had a "passion for sitting outdoors under cover during thunderstorms, and it turns out that this building bears a striking resemblance to the Thunder House in her garden at Munstead Wood."

From inside the structure, one can view the next level, ten feet below, with a terrace scooped from the surrounding woodland. The design is rectilinear, with a lawn bordered in perimeter walks and a loggia at the far end. Beyond and below the Thunder House is a square pond with a fountain overflowing into a rill that leads to a central, rectangular lily pond. The atmosphere at this Tranquility Pool is cool and restful.

Walking through the garden, one repeatedly encounters rustic stone embellishments in the paths, water features, and walls. These carefully crafted patterns of circles, squares, fans, and frames were borrowed from Jekyll's work, both in style and in the material used. Some are made of ironstone, a small, dark, flat rock found in the topsoil throughout the garden. Others are made of honey-colored Bargate stone cobbles, which the Thompsons saved from demolition at the beginning of their project.

In the spring, the wooded property is alight with 700,000 flowering bulbs. It also includes a kitchen and cut flower garden with a repurposed shipping container shed, a natural fish pond with an overhanging deck, and a fire pit in a grove of thirty-foot-tall laurels, with benches made from oak trees that were removed during construction.

OPPOSITE A grass path runs through an allée of pleached *Tilia platyphyllos* 'Rubra', underplanted with hellebore, *Geranium nodosum*, and *Allium hollandicum* 'Purple Sensation'.

The generous stone walk that leads to the Thunder House is bordered by
clusters of catmint interspersed with hardy geraniums and roses.

FROM TOP In the Reception Garden, shade-loving hostas, ferns, and heucheras planted in raised beds surround a tiered fountain, with pretty *Erigeron karvinskianus* planted below. • Border plantings in soft colors include a luscious combination of Cottage Rose (*Rosa* 'Ausglisten'), *Nepeta racemosa* 'Walker's Low', and *Stachys byzantina* 'Silver Carpet'.

RIGHT The Thunder House overlooks the Tranquility Pool terrace.

Pettifers Garden

LOWER WARDINGTON, OXFORDSHIRE

FEW GARDENS ARE MORE APT to inspire than Pettifers. Owner and creator Gina Price started with little knowledge of how to make a garden, but over the years she has developed a persistent attitude of wanting to make it better. Her restless perfectionism has turned a typical townhouse plot into an exceptional garden.

Within a structure of crisp rectangles, Gina has created plantings that celebrate color, movement, and seasonality. A trip to India inspired a shift to a brighter, purer palette and a fearless approach to color combinations, including acid yellow with punches of purple and shocking pink with fiery orange.

Dutch garden designer Piet Oudolf's use of grasses was another inspiration. After Gina became aware of the advantages of using these more dynamic plants, she removed many shrubs in the garden and planted *Cortaderia richardii*, *Calamagrostis ×acutiflora* 'Avalanche', and *Miscanthus sinensis* 'Yakushima Dwarf' in their place. Offering year-round interest, these grasses contribute heavily to late-season structure and vibrancy in the garden.

Situated in a small Oxfordshire village, Pettifers offers little hint from the street of what lies behind Gina's golden stone house. Entering through a side gate, visitors must take a few steps and pivot to the left to appreciate the genius of the garden. A long panel of lawn draws the eye to the gently rolling countryside rising beyond. This distinctly English pastoral view makes the garden feel warm and open and, like all borrowed landscapes, makes it appear much larger than it actually is.

From this vantage point, the garden falls away and the bottom is out of sight. The levels next to the house are intimate and low, with a diamond-patterned center path of granite and gravel. Weathered dry stone piers mark the way forward, as the path descends through two sets of half-moon–shaped steps to the large, rectangular lawn flanked by borders in which Gina weaves her color magic.

Farther down is a wide parterre, which Gina calls "a garden within a garden," where four yew topiaries shaped as stylized chess pieces stand as sentries. This is not a traditional parterre with an internal pattern. Instead, it is a boxwood-enclosed modern mix of domed topiaries in no discernible arrangement,

with roses, clematis, dahlias, agapanthus, yarrow, eryngium, eucomis, and alstroemerias.

In spring, the lawn around the parterre is brimming with lavender, white, and pale-yellow crocuses, followed by blue anemones and pink and white fritillaries. The grass is not cut until early summer to protect these beauties in her Botticelli Meadow. Other areas near the parterre include the Burgundy Border, the Klimt Border, the Autumn Border, and beyond a rustic gate, the Paddock.

With the aid of Polly Stevens, a highly skilled full-time gardener, Gina continually edits, discarding languishing plants, repeating star performers, and adding the latest exciting finds. In her *Pettifers Garden Blog*, Gina once mused, "Walking round the garden . . . three thoughts went tumbling through my mind. Structure, atmosphere, and most important, the ability to change your mind."

Long-blooming *Kniphofia* 'Sunningdale Yellow' steals the show in a border with late-summer perennials and grasses.

OPPOSITE In early summer, a mown path leads through the rough grass of the Botticelli Meadow, which protects ripening crocus, anemone, and fritillarias.

A rosy glow bathes a planting of dictamnus, *Allium hollandicum* 'Purple Sensation', phlomis, and barberry at dawn, creating an alluring contrast to the dense shapes of the topiary in the parterre.

In the fall, the vibrant, yellow-gold leaves of *Betula ermanii* are the focus in the lower garden.

FROM TOP Gina illustrates her love of clear, rich colors by combining achilleas, kniphofias, veronicastrums, and echinaceas in the Klimt Border. • *Cornus alternifolia* 'Argentea' visually marks the transition from the more intimate areas close to the house to the expansive lawn flanked by colorful borders.

The Barn

SERGE HILL, ABBOTS LANGLEY, HERTFORDSHIRE

TOM STUART-SMITH is one of Britain's most admired garden designers. He is best known for his large, modern country gardens where the structure is formal and the plantings are intensely naturalistic and romantic. Perched on a Hertfordshire hilltop just thirty minutes by train from London is his own garden, The Barn, where he hones his prodigious horticultural skills.

Tom's garden offers lovely views over fields, hedgerows, and woods. This has been his testing ground and inspiration since he and his wife, Sue, designed it in 1989. A few years prior, when they moved to the seventeenth-century, renovated, timber-framed barn, the surrounding land was suitable for farming but otherwise empty even of trees. Now the garden includes about half an acre of ornamental gardens, six acres of native wildflower meadows, and, since 2011, a half-acre exotic prairie planted with mainly North American plants.

Visitors first enter a courtyard enclosed on three sides by the barn, with the remaining side made of a long, rusty Corten steel wall. A U-shaped terrace at the house level extends around the building and overlooks the scene. The courtyard, always visible through the large barn windows, has a simple, linear design with cobblestone paths connecting two small terraces set with spare, black furniture, where the couple and their three children can relax. The sunny, south-facing garden is enlivened by raised Corten steel tanks filled to the brim with reflective, still water. The materials used for all these elements were recycled from Tom's 2006 Chelsea Flower Show garden, which was awarded Best of Show.

Flowers begin blooming in late winter, with snowdrops, then dwarf narcissus and jewel-toned tulips, before transitioning to a rich, complex palette of perennials and grasses. Ruby-red astrantias flower alongside copper-colored irises. Salvias, echinaceas, and heleniums intermingle with *Stipa arundinacea* and *S. calamagrostis*. In midsummer, when the slender, arching, green twigs of the *Genista aetnensis* are bursting with bright yellow, pealike flowers, the courtyard is filled with a luminous glow.

Behind the barn is the West Garden, where a series of hedged spaces is connected by grass paths. A dining terrace just outside the back doors looks over the area, surrounded by irregularly shaped, cloud-pruned yews, with a soft ridge at the top of each rounded shape, indicating the playfulness in Tom's design. His signature exuberantly mixed perennials and grasses are densely planted, a little wild, and often quite tall. Foxtail lilies, plume poppies, and mulleins reach skyward. Says Tom, who is more than six feet tall, "I wasn't really made to be an admirer of pebble-sized saxifrages and have always loved plants that look me in the face" (Donald 2011).

Farther on, crisply-cut hornbeams frame rectangular spaces of lawn. The unadorned spaces offer a striking contrast to the complexity of other garden areas, enabling one to shift perspective from the vitality of the highly designed garden to the quietness of the cultivated landscape in the Native Meadow beyond.

In 1990, a year after they created the structure of the gardens around the house, the Stuart-Smiths sowed seeds by hand for their native wildflower meadow. In late summer, the meadow is cut for hay and requires very little else for the rest of the year. Mown paths arc through the soothing planting, encouraging exploration.

One path curves to the east and ends at the Exotic Prairie, developed in 2011. Tom worked with Professor James Hitchmough from the University of Sheffield, an expert in sowing meadows and prairies, to determine the seed mix and set up a planting regime for the area. In late summer and fall, the meadow is in full flower, with colorful waves of rudbeckia, aster, silphium, liatris, echinacea, *Dianthus carthusianorum*, and *Eryngium yuccifolium*. This prairie requires considerably less maintenance than a typical garden. "All gardens are manipulated spaces, but in this prairie, there is a sense that you have just enabled it," Tom said. "There is no design beyond the seed mix. It is an encounter with nature" (Jones 2015).

In 2011, Tom was the subject of a retrospective exhibition at the Garden Museum in London, for which a video was made. The final words in the film, spoken by Sue, suggest what the garden has come to mean to them after thirty years of tending: "The garden is a resource, a repository of beauty, something to turn to when tired and empty. It gives back more than it takes."

OPPOSITE Rudbeckia, aster, and *Eryngium yuccifolium* serve up a feast for pollinators in the Exotic Prairie, which frequently holds its colors until late October.

A stepped, grass path, bordered by *Stipa calamagrostis* and *Macleaya cordata* (plume poppy), leads through a series of hedged garden rooms in the West Garden.

FROM TOP The dining patio overlooks the West Garden, with perennial borders planted in Tom's exuberantly naturalistic style. • Tall columns of *Taxus baccata* 'Fastigiata' have a noble presence in a border with low-clipped boxwood hedges, phlox, nepeta, allium, and euphorbia.

The graceful, small Mediterranean trees, *Genista aetnensis*,
light up the courtyard when they explode into bloom.

Wildside

BUCKLAND MONACHORUM, DEVON

WHAT MAKES THE NATURALISTIC GARDEN at Wildside unique, says owner Keith Wiley, "is the combination of extensive land-forming . . . with sympathetic planting." From a gently sloping, four-acre apple orchard, the visionary plantsman and his late wife, Ros, molded the land into hillocks and valleys, steep slopes and deep ravines, and sun-drenched ridges and shady hollows. "In total, I estimate I have personally moved close to 110,000 tons of material to create Wildside, all with a [mini] digger and dumper," he says matter-of-factly.

In 2004, the Wileys purchased the land that was to become Wildside after twenty-five years at The Garden House just a half-mile away. Keith had been the much-admired head gardener there, and under his stewardship, The Garden House became one of the most innovative and respected gardens in England. Looking for a way to break the strictures of traditional gardening (the flower border, for example), he began interpreting ideas he noticed in natural landscapes from around the world, modifying them to suit local conditions. "I wasn't trying to copy what I had seen in nature but [rather making] an attempt to capture the flavor or essence of somewhere I had seen that had touched me emotionally," he explains.

He has maintained this design aesthetic in the creation of Wildside. In the beginning, there were no plans to show how the garden would be organized or where thousands of plants, which the Wileys had brought with them from the nursery at The Garden House, would be placed. His vision was simply to create areas throughout the garden that offered similar conditions to the plants' natural environments in the wild.

The inspiration for the ferocious effort at Wildside came from Keith's close study of plants in wild landscapes, where he absorbed the subtleties of habitat, microclimate, and topography. Instead of matching plants to existing conditions, as most gardeners do, he creates the conditions that the plants need, a topsy-turvy version of "right plant, right place."

Until her death in April 2019, Ros played a vital role as a supporter and helper. She tended plants in the nursery, assisted with maintenance, and, above all, acted as a sounding board for her husband's ideas. As a painter, she found the ever-changing supply of painting subjects at her doorstep endlessly exciting and inspiring.

Over a period of years, as the earthworks took shape, the couple decided that the lower garden, with its gently undulating hills and valleys, would be home to their collection of Japanese maples, wisterias, magnolias, and flowering dogwoods. Planted in small copses, these trees and shrubs are underplanted with woodland plants from around the world.

The middle one-third acre around the new house is a walled courtyard garden, with a wisteria pergola and a collection of plants native to semiarid zones of the world. Conifers such as *Fitzroya cupressoides* and *Cupressus cashmeriana* were included here because they are similar in shape to conifers in California's Joshua Tree National Park and Utah's Bryce Canyon, both special places for Keith. A carefully pruned grove of *Elaeagnus* 'Quicksilver' resembles a grove of olive trees in the Mediterranean. Spikey outlines of yuccas, libertias, watsonias, and dieramas accentuate the semiarid design, as do repeated clumps of santolinas, interspersed with agapanthus and species gladioli. The low-growing grasses *Nassella tenuissima* and *N. trichotoma* provide softer forms that tie it all together.

Behind the courtyard on higher ground are the Canyons, an area that is still being developed. Birch trees grow on the rocky banks, and there are plans for a shallow, meandering, rock-strewn stream to course through the open center, which is surrounded by dramatic gorges and cliffs planted with agapanthus, crocosmia, dierama, and kniphofia. Here Keith intends to re-create the natural areas he visited in South Africa, with a bit of the Mojave Desert thrown in.

The work is not yet finished. There are ponds to refine in the large water garden, summerhouses to build with important vistas, and native plants to add to the highest summit connecting the garden to the countryside. But for the visitor looking out over the lower garden and the courtyard, the Wileys' vision has been actualized. The landscape here appears natural, like it has always been so, a layered terrain with folds and furrows, richly gardenesque, half hidden, and beckoning one to explore.

OPPOSITE *Elaeagnus* 'Quicksilver' shrubs trained as small trees add vigorous notes to colorful perennials and feathery grasses.

Keith's planting style is best described as a wild naturalism with an intuitive use of repetition and rhythm in texture and color.

In July, Keith's hand-built banks are an enchanting, painterly haven covered
with an explosion of flowers from the tips of one's toes to above one's head.

ABOVE Autumn-blooming colchicums add fresh sparks of color under a group of apple trees in the center of the lower garden.

LEFT Salvias, kniphofias, and grasses create vertical contrasts to mounding *Coreopsis verticillata* 'Zagreb' and santolinas.

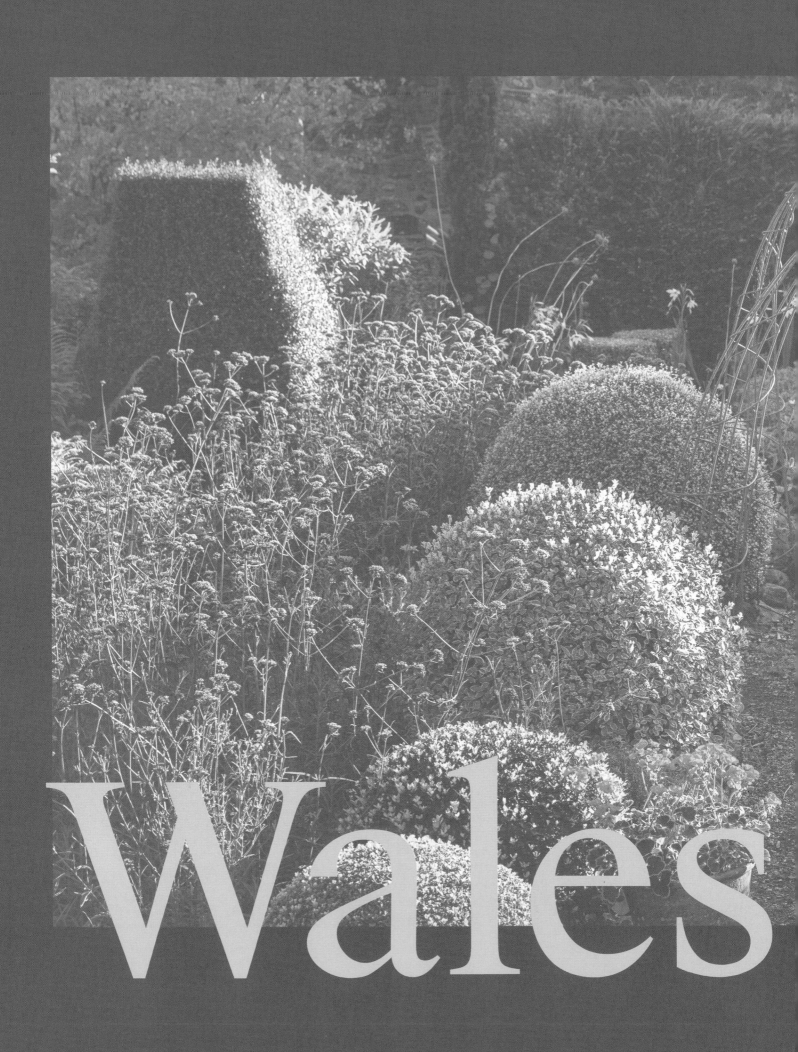

Wales

Dyffryn Fernant Gardens

FISHGUARD, PEMBROKESHIRE

WHEN ONE SURVEYS THE GARDENS at Dyffryn Fernant, it's impossible to believe that the property was a veritable wilderness when Christina Shand and David Allum moved there in 1996. Impenetrable brambles, blackthorn, and Japanese knotweed covered the neglected six-acre farm. Christina hoped to create modest gardens, with prized plants in the front and vegetables in the back, but when she began clearing the land, she discovered it was half rocks and half bog. Thus began her resolute journey to discover how to garden on this challenging land.

Located a mile from the Irish Sea, the windswept property is located under the Preseli uplands in southwestern Wales, notable for being a source for some of the gigantic stones used at Stonehenge. The garden, which surrounds the couple's stone farmhouse painted coral pink, was made with deep respect for this particular spot. The design is contemporary yet attached to the past, naturalistic yet in places stylized and exotic. "At no point did I want to 'lay down' a garden on the surface," says Christina. "This garden has been designed within the spaces already offered by the old farm walls, the presence of a wild marsh, and the fact that it was overlooked by uncultivated rocky slopes."

During the past twenty-four years, Christina has developed eighteen separate garden spaces, some with drolly open-ended names, such as The Between and The Beyond. The Front Garden is less ambiguous. Hugging the rose-draped house, the garden is densely planted in radiant colors and robust textures. Plants spill from every nook and cranny, and dozens of pots add seasonal color with plants that would not otherwise thrive here. A waist-high, dry stone wall defines this inner entry garden bisected by a cobble-and-stone path leading to the front door. On top of the wall, a carved wooden sculpture by the late John Cleal shares space with glass fishing floats and smooth, round stones. Off to the side is a small, circular patio paved with irregular stones, with a portly copper brandy still in the center, which the couple converted into a water basin. In late summer, the garden features the brilliant jewel tones of potted dahlias.

Across the way in the Courtyard, Christina plays audaciously with form, texture, and contrast. Agaves in terracotta pots accent the gravel path, surrounded by the bold structures of tetrapanax, acanthus, ricinus, melianthus, and cannas. Containers provide Christina with opportunities for flexible arrangements of plants and carefully chosen sculptural and found objects. At eye level, willowy miscanthus and spiny artichoke tower over eucomis, sedum, bronze-leaved sedge, and elegant white agapanthus. "The garden has taught me that I have a naturally artistic eye," she says, "and [it] has been a great pleasure indulging and developing this."

In the Orchard, a blowsy, late-summer double border of actea, helianthus, crocosmia, and persicaria are punctuated with the occasional fruit tree. In the Rickyard, clipped orbs of gray and green evergreen shrubs are juxtaposed with lavender *Verbena bonariensis*, purple-black aeoniums, and red pelargoniums.

A little farther out, Christina took advantage of the naturally occurring wetland and created a Bog Garden. Before the jungle of plants reaches its summer peak, the standout feature here is a striking stainless steel obelisk made by David. Bright pink primula flowers make way for lighter filipendula blooms. As temperatures rise, so do the flower stalks of acanthus, gunneras, and calla lilies. Beyond the cultivated spaces, a pond and marsh on the property are less tamed, and the garden boundary merges into the native terrain. "My biggest success," says Christina, "is blending with the landscape."

By offering a wide variety of garden environments and plenty of places to sit and contemplate, she hopes visitors will feel delighted and inspired, and perhaps calmed and healed. Christina learned to garden by reading the books of renowned English gardeners Christopher Lloyd and Beth Chatto, and she generously offers a library of gardening books to share with guests while they enjoy a cup of tea.

OPPOSITE The couple created a water basin from an old copper brandy still.

Colorful dahlias brighten the Front Garden in late summer.

FROM TOP Christina has artfully arranged stones and jugs around stone troughs planted with succulents, black mondo grass, and other small plant treasures. • A gravel path leads through the Courtyard, which is filled with exotic architectural plants and carefully chosen sculptural and found objects. • In the Rickyard, a playful, rustic arch creates a casual statement among sphere-shaped *Pittosporum tenuifolium* 'Irene Paterson', *Verbena bonariensis*, and potted red pelargoniums.

Where two paths cross in the middle of the Bog Garden is a crisp obelisk, a reflective vertical accent amid a vigorous planting of canna, darmera, dierama, and zantedeschia.

Veddw

DEVAUDEN, MONMOUTHSHIRE

WHEN ANNE WAREHAM CAME TO VEDDW in 1987 with her husband, Charles Hawes, she was determined to make a garden that wasn't simply beautiful; it also needed, in the deepest sense, to be of its place, to be thought-provoking, and to have meaning. With what Anne calls their "bloody-minded fanaticism," she and Charles have created a garden that realizes her vision.

Located on a slope hollowed out of woodland in a small valley in southeastern Wales, the two acres at Veddw presented a daunting undertaking. After visiting other gardens and consulting a number of gardening books, Anne sorted out her likes (geometric structures and lines) from her dislikes (wiggly paths and random plantings) and developed the confidence to begin creating her dream.

The garden's meaning came to light as she researched the area's history and the people who had lived there over the centuries—the cottage farmers who eked out a living there. The land emotionally connected Anne to those hardscrabble lives. "It's hard to explain the excitement I feel to stand somewhere and think of the people who have lived, worked, created, built and rebuilt on that very same piece of land or in that very building over thousands of years" (Wareham 2017).

Visitors enter Veddw at the very top of a slope, where they immediately see how the garden and house relate to the site and how the site relates to the agricultural valley beyond. Behind the house is a semicircle of native oak and beech trees that form a graceful backdrop for the bowl-shaped gardens. A handmade bench faces the garden, its clay-colored, curving back inscribed with various ways Veddw has been spelled over the centuries.

Ahead on the downward slope is the Grasses Parterre, with irregular spaces edged in low boxwood and filled with a variety of ornamental grasses. The parterre's design, based on an 1841 tithe map, was created as an homage to the field boundaries of the local landscape and the people who toiled there.

Beyond the parterre is a network of mazelike, linear hedges, many above eye level, most with deep green foliage. Some of the hedges are topped with refined curves that reflect the rolling hills of the adjacent landscape. The hedges form walls in a warren of rooms connected by narrow paths that culminate in a dramatic reflecting pool, where black water mirrors the elegantly shaped hedges that rise behind it like overlapping waves.

Not far away is a gate that opens into the woods. It is painted black and inscribed in gold with writings by a nineteenth-century local schoolmaster, who tells of the "small farmers, quarrymen, woodcutters, and laborers" who lived in the area and their meager rations and poverty. In her book, *The Bad Tempered Gardener*, Anne expresses hope that this tribute will remind visitors "of other lives lived out so very differently" (Wareham 2011) from their own.

Closer to the house, both in front and in back, plantings are more flowery and less restrained, with favored perennials repeated or gathered into masses. Blowsy *Campanula lactiflora* abounds in one border, and *Chamaenerion angustifolium* 'Stahl Rose' cavorts in another. Statuesque, silvery cardoons loom over purplish heucheras. Self-seeding *Alchemilla mollis* romps around a little pond, and the stones in a terrace are laced with playful *Erigeron* 'Profusion' and wispy *Nassella tenuissima*. The effect is unexpectedly romantic.

Making the gardens at Veddw has had a profound effect on the couple. Charles has become a photographer and Anne a writer, both focusing on gardens. Their deep understanding of this place and their commitment to expressing their concerns and preoccupations through its design became a successful combination. More than anything, Veddw is about them, their hearts and minds.

A painted wooden fence suggests a city skyline.

OPPOSITE From the Grasses Parterre, one can view the surrounding bucolic countryside.

Behind the dramatic reflecting pool, clipped *Taxus baccata* hedges rise toward the natural woodland.

The back garden features yew hedges trimmed in wavy shapes that reflect the surrounding hills.

OPPOSITE, FROM TOP In the Front Garden, *Euphorbia griffithii* 'Fireglow', *Cotinus coggygria* 'Grace', and crocosmia surround a birdbath made of mild steel on a wooden plinth. • Stainless steel mirror globes mounted on wooden posts make striking vertical statements in the sloping meadow dotted with *Camassia leichtlinii* subsp. *leichtlinii*.

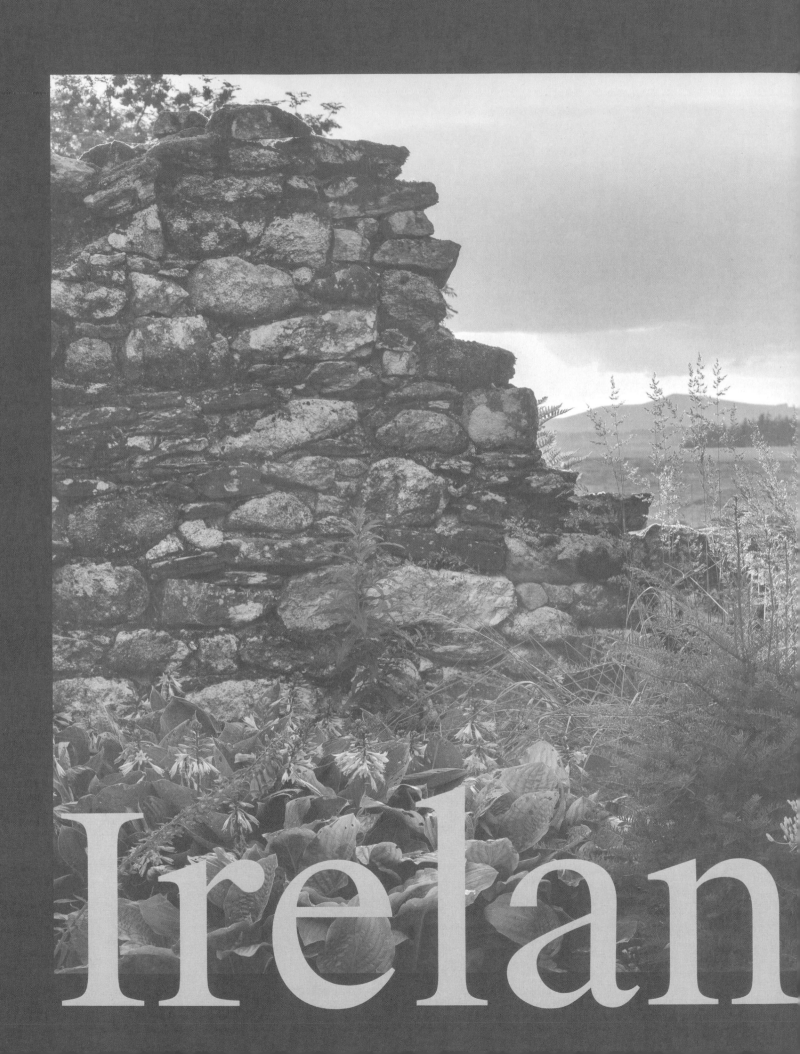

Irelan

d

Caher Bridge Garden

FORMOYLE WEST, BALLYVAUGHAN, COUNTY CLARE

THE LIMESTONE PLATEAUS of County Clare on Ireland's west coast are sometimes described as lunarlike, unforgiving, and bleak. The glaciated karst landscape of the Burren, an Anglicization of the Gaelic for "a place of stone," is bounded by the Atlantic Ocean and Galway Bay. This undulating landscape is covered in endless sheets of pale, gray limestone, sometimes 1600 feet thick, pocked and rutted by eons of rain. "It's wet, windy, and virtually soil free," remarks Carl Wright. "The conditions here are about as difficult as it gets." And he should know, because he made his garden here.

Carl, an ecologist, vacationed in the area as a child and returned as a young man to work in a neighboring village. In 1996, he bought a derelict stone cottage and twelve acres next to a bridge over the Caher River, near the village of Fanore. He spent the next three years rebuilding every inch of the cottage interior.

Outside the cottage, the property was scattered with stone rubble and wild thickets of hazel, black-thorn, and hawthorn. When he began clearing the scrub to add a front path, he discovered that almost no soil existed over the limestone. At that time, however, he was not concerned because he wanted to leave the place wild.

Several years later, when Carl noticed water fill-ing a large hole he'd dug next to the river in which to bury debris, he saw that this would be an ideal place for a pond. This realization sparked a latent interest in creating a garden, and by 2003, he had quit his job, dedicating all his time to building a garden that would blend into its environment.

Carl has incorporated many of the existing scrub species and wildflowers into his garden, along with a considerable number of native plants. He linked the pond directly to the river, extending the existing water habitat to accommodate wildlife. Using the limestone on the property, he hand-built walls, ter-races, paths, steps, and windows—all constructed with impressive craftsmanship.

Today's almost two-and-a-half acre garden is designed in a curvilinear fashion. Carl has frequently used the double stone arches in the Caher Bridge to scale the circular elements he creates. He has also indulged his love of plants by collecting nota-ble groups of snowdrops, daffodils, daylilies, ferns, and hostas.

The shady front garden offers views to the pond, the river, the bridge, and the stony face of the Burren in the distance. A double-sided dry stone wall fronts the road. Hazels have been pruned into small, multi-stemmed trees, and a hawthorn shelters the front door. Snowdrops, daffodils, and hellebores signal the arrival of spring weeks before the hostas in the terracotta pots along the shaded house walls begin to push up their lusty leaves.

At the side of the house, a wooden gate opens to the back garden, where the design is more complex, with serpentine retaining walls raising the plantings above the porous limestone that underlies every square foot. Carl backfilled each wall with imported soil that he painstakingly picked clean of all seeds before planting. By his calculations, he has built a mile of stone walls and wheelbarrowed in at least 1400 tons of soil.

Roses are trained on this sunnier side of the house, and a small lawn is surrounded by blossoms in lively colors and lovely scents. Farther on, a handsome, stone-built moon window, with a small circular pond below, signals a transition into dappled woodland of native ash, hazel, and holly. Raised beds filled with ferns, primroses, geraniums, and brunneras rim terraces and line meandering paths. Steps lead up the slope into shady, moist thickets, which eventually open to a meadow dotted with Irish daffodils, camassias, and hawthorns.

Carl has planted more than forty different bergenias at Caher Bridge, and he has collected twenty-two cultivars of *Brunnera macrophylla*—small collections compared to the one hundred fifty fern species and cultivars he has planted throughout the garden. A longtime collector of primroses (he has so many that he has lost count), he is particularly fond of those that are Irish in origin.

Spring is Carl's favorite season, when new growth is frenzied, the days are growing longer, and the birdsong is incredible. It reminds him that his gar-den can continue to evolve and that he will be able to share it again with visitors. The immense pleasure of making new friends and contacts brought about by his garden inspires him to continue his efforts, despite the difficult conditions of the Burren.

OPPOSITE FROM TOP Carl built this extraordinary moon window using stones he collected on the site. • Dry stone walls backfilled with clean soil brought in by wheelbarrow allow Carl to grow a wide variety of plants such as *Dierama igneum*, a glorious pink-flowering South African native.

CLOCKWISE FROM TOP LEFT A red-leaved, moisture-loving *Rodgersia aesculifolia* cultivar is perched along the edge of the pond. • In spring, the striking, white-and-blue flowers of *Brunnera macrophylla* 'Henry's Eyes' appear. • The shade-loving primrose Belarina Amethyst Ice grows in the dappled woodland. • Carl has planted more than forty different bergenias in his garden, including *Bergenia* 'Diamond Drops'.

Hunting Brook Gardens

LAMB HILL, BLESSINGTON, COUNTY WICKLOW

IN THE FOOTHILLS of the Wicklow Mountains, southwest of Dublin, is Hunting Brook Gardens, which Jimi Blake calls a "crazy collection of plants from all over the world." Each year, Jimi travels for several months to far-flung places, bringing back whatever plants excite him. His garden represents one of Ireland's largest private plant collections, with ever-evolving spaces where he experiments to his heart's content. Despite his tongue-in-cheek description, Jimi has made a sophisticated landscape filled with painterly plant vignettes, deftly designed to feature color, texture, contrast, and rhythm.

Jimi's parents gave him this twenty-acre section of the family farm in 2003. On one side, a sloping sheep pasture opened to a view over meadows to the mountains. On the other side, the pasture backed up to a wooded ravine with a stream. Later, on a nineteenth-century map, Jimi found the stream called Hunting Brook, which prompted him to name his garden in its honor. By 2005, he had built a modest timber house on the property, and he welcomed visitors to his gardens.

Early gardens in the sunny areas around Jimi's house featured large sweeps of late-season grasses and perennials inspired by the designs of Oehme, van Sweden, an American landscape architecture firm. Jimi, restlessly curious and energetic, has made many changes. "I need to be fired up about my garden so I'm always changing it," he explains. Today, he calls his approach "a modern fusion of meadow style and tropical planting."

His blend of meadow and tropical is most clearly expressed in the middle of the garden at the front of the house. Bold leaves of *Canna* 'Taney', *Musa sikkimensis* 'Bengal Tiger', *Colocasia esculenta* 'Pink China', and *Cyphomandra betacea* emerge above perennials and annuals that include dahlias, sanguisorbas, salvias, and marigolds, in an energetic, textural display.

Recently, in the main border leading to the house, Jimi completely redesigned the beds with lower, simpler plantings that provide open views to the surrounding countryside. Here, the pastel-orange tones of *Geum* 'Totally Tangerine', *Linaria* 'Peachy', and apricot-colored *Sphaeralcea* 'Childerley' mingle with dark, reddish bronze *Aeonium* 'Cyclops', ruby-red *Centaurea atropurpurea*, and chartreuse *Euphorbia rigida*. Woven through are breezy *Stipa barbata* and *Nassella tenuissima*, which add movement to the scheme. As a final touch, he added hundreds of calendulas—*Calendula* 'Bronze Beauty' and *C. officinalis* 'Zeolights'.

Behind the house, a narrow path winds into the steeply sloping woodland, where the atmosphere is quiet, damp, and cool—a dramatic change from the intensity near the house. In the dappled shade of tall oaks, sycamores, and larches, Jimi features his beloved architectural foliage plants. Pseudopanax, schefflera, fatsia, and cordyline are planted with *Valeriana pyrenaica*, ferns, foxgloves, hardy begonias, and Solomon's seal.

At the bottom of the ravine, where the path crosses the mossy edged, burbling stream, is an oversized, rustic wooden table and benches—like an enchanted forest scene in a fairy tale. From the ravine, steep steps lead up the other side and into a large, open meadow with broad views to the Wicklow Mountains. A curving, mown path leads to a single standing stone, a reminder that this ancient land once belonged to a Bronze Age settlement.

At one time, Jimi, being a consummate collector, wanted more than anything to test his growing skills with obscure, difficult plants. But over the years, he has changed his goal: He wants to ensure that Hunting Brook looks good from early spring until the first hard frost. To that end, he seeks out the very best, longest flowering perennials to combine with superior foliage plants, an endeavor that is both modern and inventive.

OPPOSITE *Cleistocactus strausii*, *Calendula officinalis* 'Indian Prince', and echeveria cultivars grow along the entrance walk. Jimi brings the cacti into his house in the winter and replants them outdoors in spring.

FROM TOP *Kniphofia* 'Fiery Fred', *Linaria* 'Peachy', and *Geum* 'Totally Tangerine' set off *Nassella tenuissima* in the emerging dawn light. • Tiny buttercups and allium globes fill the meadow between the house and the woodland in late spring.

LEFT Spires of *Verbascum thapsus* and vibrant blossoms of *Geum* 'Totally Tangerine' stand out vividly among other perennials and grasses in the early morning light.

June Blake's Garden

TINODE, BLESSINGTON, COUNTY WICKLOW

AN HOUR SOUTHWEST of Dublin in the middle of sheep country is June Blake's contemporary, formal, and intensely naturalistic three-acre garden. Though self-trained, June possesses formidable gardening instincts and a sharp designer's eye for detail.

In the front lawn of her granite steward's cottage, built in the 1860s, a curved path winds between gentle landforms and ends in a shady border filled to the brim with rodgersias, ferns, astrantias, and pulmonarias in a dreamy color blend of bronzes, dusty pinks, and silvers. At the border's end, a low-hanging larch branch leans into June's main garden, which is filled with glorious blossoms in every shape and color imaginable.

Dry stone walls created mostly from local shale raise each flower-filled bed to eye level, enveloping the viewer in sensuous plantings. Dotted throughout the beds are multistemmed *Aralia echinocaulis*, their height changing the garden's skyline and their thin canopies casting a light shade. Glowing, vertical stems of timber bamboo divert attention from the finer textures and vivid colors of perennials.

At the end of the formal beds are turf steps formed from railroad ties that lead through a small meadow to a viewing mound at the top of the garden, where the garden's overall structure is revealed. A grid of seven rectangles, each bounded by generous six-foot-wide gravel paths, aligns with key elements in the architecture of the cottage. From this vantage point, the plantings converge into a living painting, with colors and textures merging and mingling in the light.

From here, a curving, ramped lawn path leads down to the main garden, offering changing views out over the garden as one descends. Halfway down the minimalist, rectangular reflecting pool is revealed, framed in a band of cobblestone found on site. On one side, an old, shoulder-high granite wall holds back the hillside. At either end of the pool, the modern theme is accentuated with angular, polished concrete benches that create places of calm in a sea of color and texture.

June encourages contemplation in her garden. In the middle of her exuberant plantings, she has added a stark, sunken, enclosed sitting space. Here, she offers a different garden perspective. By eschewing plants entirely in this space, she hopes visitors will focus upward on the sky and treetops.

Early May is June's favorite time in the garden, when tulips are in bloom and she is encouraged by the promise of everything to follow. Each autumn, she prepares for the upcoming spring season by planting 8000 tulips in a range of saturated colors—from the darkest of purples, maroons, and reds, to sprinklings of spicy orange. In spring, the tulips bloom beside the lime-greens of *Polygonatum verticillatum*, coral-red *Euphorbia griffithii* 'Dixter', and golden-hued *Chionochloa rubra*, along with blossoms of peonies and rodgersias. It is a colorist's fantasy.

A low-hanging larch branch stretches above hardy geraniums, alchemilla, yarrow, and veronicastrum.

OPPOSITE The vibrant, vertical stems of *Phyllostachys vivax* 'Aureocaulis' contrast strikingly with underplanted perennials in pink, burgundy, and orange.

The reflecting pool adds a serene, modern note in this colorful garden.

June plants thousands of tulips in the autumn in anticipation of an
explosion of color in early May, her favorite time of year.

Multistemmed *Aralia echinocaulis* provide vertical accents in the perennial beds.

A flowering dogwood is surrounded by a lavish profusion of alliums, ferns, euphorbias, astrantias, hardy geraniums, blue-flowering poppies, foxgloves, and rodgersia.

Sheilstown

KNOCKANANNA, COUNTY WICKLOW

IN 2002, Dominick Murphy purchased Sheilstown, a derelict nineteenth-century farmhouse on fourteen acres in the Wicklow Mountains. For three years, he renovated the house before moving there from Dublin to address the outdoors. "A key underpinning for Sheilstown," explains Dominick, "is not to tame the wildness of nature around me, but to work with it, to place a garden in that space and context, to allow plants to create their own wild ecosystems, and not try to control or tame them."

Raised in a creative family steeped in the arts, Dominick chose gardens as his aesthetic medium and became a horticulturist and landscape designer, starting Murphy + Sheanon with his business partner, Colum Sheanon. At Sheilstown, Dominick wanted the atmosphere to be that of an Irish hilltop farm. "The garden must be authentic to its place," he says. Sheilstown is "deeply set into its agricultural context, on the side of a mountain, that gets extreme weather." He was not interested in imposing a design on the site.

"My garden is a naturalistic, wild garden," he explains. "I've tried to take the garden back to less, and to do 'more of less.'" Now that it's mature, Sheilstown reveals itself slowly as one walks along paths that veer and curve throughout the garden. Visitors forge their own journeys, discovering their own versions of the place. Paths are bounded by tousled plantings, a reminder that he does not intend "to tame the wildness of nature" here.

Throughout the garden, he has created visual connections to the countryside by building openings in plantings, hedgerows, and stone walls to provide views of the greater landscape. He incorporated existing granite walls and sheds, keeping the red, barrel-roofed, corrugated barn as it was. He decided that any new enclosures would be square or rectangular in shape to reflect the Irish agricultural systems of surrounding fields with wild hedgerows. He used the designs of existing iron farm gates on the property to create new ones.

Visitors enter the property via a long, gravel driveway with a grass strip down the middle. On one side, Dominick has planted a wide open, sloping meadow with native grasses and wildflowers. A broad, curving path leads visitors into the meadow, where grasses ripple in the wind and the sky seems astoundingly large. It is bounded by hawthorns with openings that allow views to the rolling landscapes of neighboring fields and the far distant mountains.

Below, at the end of the meadow, one crosses the driveway to a gravel path that leads to an ample dining terrace next to the house, paved in local sandstone. The terrace is surrounded by plantings of astrantia, ligularia, primula, and geranium, but the stars are robust clumps of *Astelia nervosa* 'Bronze Giant', with swordlike, arching leaves.

From the terrace and across a gravel farmyard, one can see the Walled Garden filled with a rambunctious mix of grasses and perennials. Partially rebuilt old granite walls enclose three sides. Here and there, Dominick has removed stones from the walls to create viewing windows that provide connections to the rolling hills. The fourth side is a raised deck set into the roofless shell of a shed next to the red barn, Dominick's favorite spot in the entire garden.

At the lowest point on the property, Dominick made a swimming pond by damming a small stream. It resembles an old-fashioned swimming hole, with frowzy plants extending to the waterline. A cantilevered, wooden deck, built from trees felled elsewhere on the property, projects over the pond's far end. Beyond are bucolic fields, lapping into one another, and in the far horizon, the softly rounded Wicklow Mountains.

OPPOSITE Dominick removed stones in the old walls to offer views into the surrounding farmland.

Along the perimeter of the dining terrace, which offers commanding views over the garden to the rural landscape, are plantings of barberries, hostas, geraniums, and robust clumps of *Astelia nervosa* 'Bronze Giant'.

FROM TOP A bench inside the Walled Garden invites visitors to rest beneath an ancient wall that has intentionally not been restored. • The cantilevered deck over the swimming pond is backed by a panoramic view of the fields and mountains.

RIGHT Near the center of the farmyard, a *Rheum palmatum* flower towers over an ebullient mix of heleniums, daylilies, and grasses.

The Dillon Garden

MONKSTOWN, COUNTY DUBLIN

IT WOULD NOT BE AN EXAGGERATION to call Helen Dillon the "queen of Irish gardening." For nearly half a century, she has captivated gardeners with her witty and opinionated writings, lectures, and television appearances. Her inspirational city garden in Ranelagh, an inner suburb of Dublin, was for many years the most-visited private garden in Ireland, and many assumed that she and this garden would always be linked.

It came as a great surprise, then, when in 2016, she and her husband, Val, an antiques dealer, announced that they were selling this much-loved house and garden and moving on. On the Dillon Garden website, Helen wrote the following: "Although we loved our Ranelagh garden to bits . . . not only was it full of old mistakes—plants which were too large, too squashed, and dare it be said, a tiny bit boring, but also the soil was old and over-used as the house was built in 1830. Thus there was a buildup of pests and diseases, from weevils to honey fungus, tulip fire, swift moth, clematis wilt and false widow spider, plus an ever increasing gang of long established slugs and snails."

The Dillons' new property in Monkstown, on Dublin Bay, is almost three times as long as it is wide. Enclosed by high, old, granite walls, the small house has been totally renovated and large windows installed to look out over the new garden. Its design includes mostly shallow beds divided by stone-edged gravel paths. At one end of the house are a green-house and an aviary for the Dillons' canaries and finch. At the other, sunnier end, a small stone terrace extends along the house and connects to a ramp that leads up to a raised area with a second greenhouse.

Visitors enter through a substantial wooden gate and within a few steps are on the long main path that parallels the house. Elegant antique urns are set prominently on pedestals at either end of the path. Plantings on either side are boldly awash with colors. "What I enjoy most now in the garden is clashing colors and dashing contrasts, with a splash of orange here and the startling scarlet of *Rosa* 'Warm Welcome' [*R.* 'Chewizz'] there, which I love but other gardeners hate," she says. "Over many years I've done blue borders, white gardens, shady green gardens, pale pink and lilac borders, and so on. Now I like the mad muddle of colors, like a box of smarties."

Using the design mantra of "cram in as many beautiful plants as possible," Helen especially enjoys siting very tall plants here and there, such as the plume poppy (*Macleaya cordata*), the giant reed (*Arundo donax*), the very uncommon *Hagenia abyssinica* tree from Ethiopia, and the bright yellow *Dendromecon rigida* from California.

One of Helen's delights in the new location has been discovering that, at 500 feet from the sea, her Monkstown garden is several degrees warmer than her old garden, and mostly frost-free. "You wouldn't believe how well my plants are looking," she said, "and stuff like quite early geraniums and alstroe-merias are virtually in flower in . . . March. It's very exciting" (*Sunday Independent* 2017). She can now happily grow the Australian mintbush (*Prostanthera ovalifolia*), the New Zealand giant forget-me-not (*Myosotidium hortensia*), and the honey bush *Melianthus major* 'Purple Haze', with its steely blue leaves tinged in moody purple.

"The longer I garden, the more I enjoy being a creator rather than a curator," she explains on the garden's website. "Very few people get the fun of starting again at my age" (*Sunday Independent* 2017).

In her long main borders, she "cram[s] in as many beautiful plants as possible."

OPPOSITE Sunny *Geum* 'Lady Stratheden' is paired with hot-pink salvia flowers, an example of Helen's enjoyment of "clashing colors and dashing contrasts."

The pendulous, yellow flowers of a brugmansia contrast with a bright orange watsonia and red double dahlia.

LEFT Helen combines fennel with cosmos, dahlias, *Eryngium ×zabelii* 'Big Blue', *Trachycarpus wagnerianus*, and *Sonchus palmensis*, her favorite thistle.

Helen has planted *Delphinium* 'Giotto' for its deep blue and violet semi-double flowers.

RIGHT Borders lining the main path are filled with *Geranium pratense* 'Plenum Violaceum', *Salvia* 'Royal Bumble', *Melianthus major* 'Antonow's Blue', *Allium* 'Globemaster', delphinium, diascia, and epilobium.

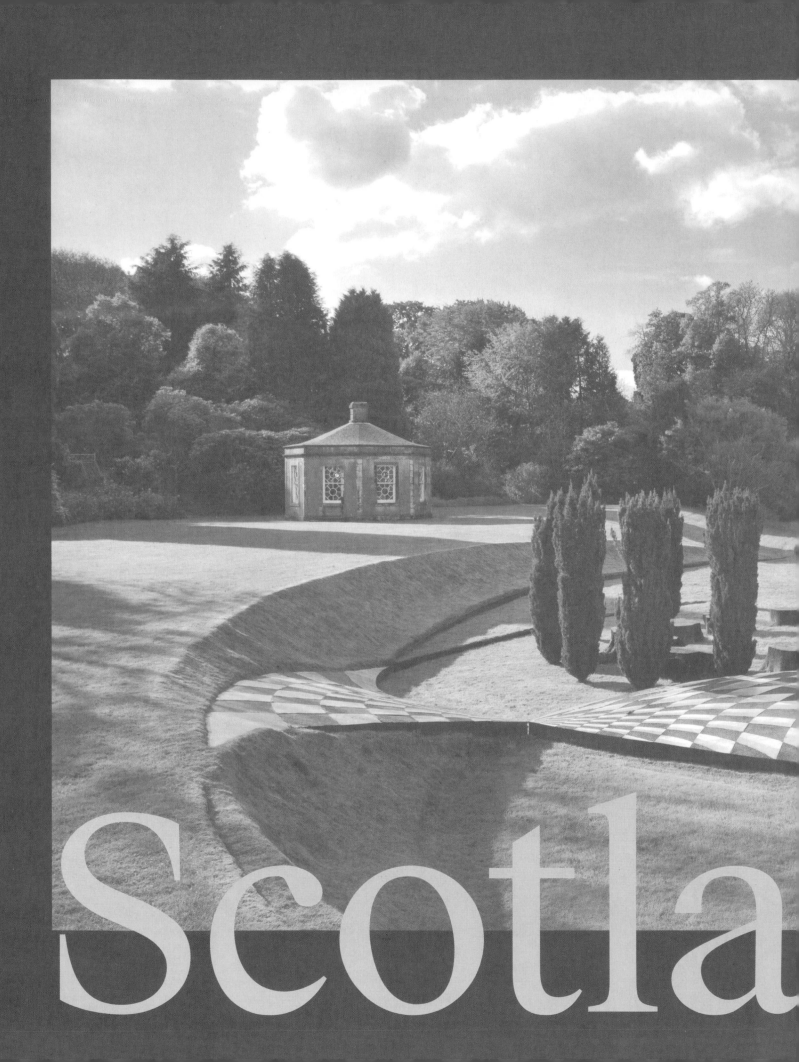

Scotla

Broadwoodside

GIFFORD, EAST LOTHIAN

ABOUT TWENTY-FIVE MILES east of Edinburgh, Broadwoodside is situated in the middle of a crazy quilt landscape of fields and woods. When Robert and Anna Dalrymple bought the property in 1997, the collection of dilapidated low stone buildings, some dating back to 1680, with a farmhouse, barns, and assorted sheds, were loosely arranged in a rectangle with openings to the surrounding fields. A few years later, after an extensive renovation, the couple had created an award-winning home and a garden filled with sharp geometry and sly wit.

During the renovation, Robert—who designs books for artists, museums, and botanical gardens and knows a thing or two about proportion and balance—drew up a comprehensive garden plan incorporating formal elements with a contemporary twist. The one-and-a-half-acre layout was partly restricted by the footprints of existing buildings and the many stone walls that surrounded them, but Robert's love of symmetry ruled the rest. His simple, straight-lined design featured some bold, geometric shapes and occasional focal-point flourishes. A central axis extended from one end of the garden to the other, creating a strong, rational sense of order on the narrow site. And that, with almost no changes, is what was built.

Because winter was coming, the couple felt some urgency regarding where to start the garden's construction. For the Dalrymples, the most important aspects of the plan were the two courtyards at the heart of the rectangle. Because many of their home's windows overlooked the courtyards, these areas would need to be engaging at all times of the year, including during the long, gray winter months.

The Upper Courtyard became a striking graphic design played out on the ground plane. Divided into a grid of twenty-five equal squares, the upper courtyard is a giant checkerboard, each square filled with grass, low evergreen plants, or granite setts. Eight of the planted squares contain *Acer platanoides* trimmed into lollipops, with each trunk featuring a metal label that drolly misidentifies the tree as a walnut, lime, willow, or birch. Near the center of the grid is the *pièce de résistance*, an impressive aviary for William, the Dalrymples' African gray parrot. Off to one side, a loggia is painted a cheery coral color with an inside wall inscription: "THE WRITING IS ON THE WALL." This garden is surely amusing, even in bad weather.

The Lower Courtyard, separated from the upper by a stone wall, is less intense in its design. Sandstone pavers rescued from an old mill were used in paths that divide a flat lawn into quarters. In the center, where the paths cross, is a collection of seasonally potted plants, anchored by a magnificent, large copper kettle. Anna has claimed this space, and because she favors a looser approach, the plantings are softer and a little wilder than those in the rest of the garden. Lining the perimeter walls are shade-loving foxgloves, Solomon's seal, astrantias, ferns, and lilies of the valley—plants that ramble and romp. A fragrant climbing 'Madame Alfred Carrière' rose adorns another wall, underplanted with cardoon, bronze fennel, and violas interrupted by statuesque clumps of *Macleaya cordata*.

Robert, who freely admits that he hates gardening, relies on the Dalrymples' highly skilled gardener, Guy Donaldson, for all the planting and maintenance. Guy has lived and worked at Broadwoodside with his family from the beginning. Regular morning meetings with Robert set his agenda and define larger goals, always recorded in a thick notebook, that keep this spirited garden on track.

Beyond the courtyards are nine named gardens, mostly linear, and all with sculptural accents—some handmade and others commissioned, but most infused with Robert's particular brand of humor. In the House Field, orbs of various materials and sizes are collected into a sculptural mound he calls *A Load of Balls*. Nearby, a stone plinth is inscribed "ORE STABIT FORTIS ARARE PLACETO RESTAT," faux Latin to be read in English for its meaning. Elsewhere, a replica of the Pompeian *Dancing Faun* statue dangles a silver yo-yo from his upraised hand. One feels the aura of Little Sparta, Ian Hamilton Finlay's poetic garden filled with ideas, words, and sculptures, albeit with a waggish twist.

OPPOSITE Rescued from a brewery that was being demolished, a cast-iron finial was repurposed as a marker for the Dog's Tomb, where the family's beloved dogs are buried.

The Upper Courtyard is based on a grid of twenty-five squares filled with alternating materials, and a well-crafted aviary for the couple's African gray parrot, William, sits in the middle.

Salvaged stone pavers form paths that divide the Lower Courtyard into quarters, with a planted copper kettle as a centerpiece.

FROM TOP The title of Robert's sculpture, *A Load of Balls*, suggests that it should not be taken too seriously. • Along a lane, a "Speed Bump" sign devolves into several anagrams.

Hopetoun House Walled Garden

SOUTH QUEENSFERRY, WEST LOTHIAN

HOPETOUN HOUSE is situated on the south shore of the estuary of the River Forth just before it flows into the North Sea. Its stately colonnaded facade overlooks a dignified eighteenth-century landscape of great formal lawns, elegantly curved drives, and dark woods. Although Edinburgh is only twelve miles away, this estate is tucked into the quiet countryside, surrounded by farmland and small villages.

On the southeast side of the house is the walled garden that once served as a kitchen garden. The tall brick walls enclose more than thirteen acres and were built in the early 1700s. But during the last dozen years, the transformation that has occurred inside those walls is very much of the twenty-first century.

In 2006, the Earl and Countess of Hopetoun were charged with overseeing the 6500-acre property after the Earl's father unexpectedly stepped aside. The change from living as a relatively normal family in London to inhabiting one of the grandest houses in Scotland naturally required some adjustments.

Lady Hopetoun, who had always gardened to some extent, decided the existing family garden on the estate was too tiny and began looking for a larger area. She wanted a space that would be private, so that she could garden and her children could play beyond the view of the house's many visitors. "It hadn't really occurred to me to take on the old walled garden," she says. "It was in such a dilapidated state and was so large, but really it was the obvious option."

Roughly rectangular in shape, the Walled Garden included a meandering stream. Farthest from the house, a woodland filled the lower garden, and the upper garden was separated by walls, hedges, or buildings into compartments that, with some far-sighted vision, she imagined would be a new garden.

From the beginning, plant choices would be the key to success: "The plants I use need to stand in winter and be very low maintenance but have appealing flower and foliage colors." There would be no deadheading or staking. She took inspiration from contemporary designers such as Piet Oudolf, Tom Stuart-Smith, and the late Henk Gerritsen.

But before any planting could begin, the soil required significant preparation. For twenty years, the upper part of the garden had been leased to a garden center for retail sales and growing areas. Much of the ground had been used for parking and was covered in stone aggregate and gravel. "The removal of this took a great deal longer and cost an awful lot more than we first anticipated," says Lady Hopetoun. After the stone and gravel were removed, she enriched the soil with tons of manure, along with seaweed gathered from the shore of the river. "Because the garden has been improved and used for almost 300 years," she notes, "the soil is actually remarkably good, with most of it now being a neutral loam."

The 5000-square-foot Old Rose Garden was the first to be revamped. Lady Hopetoun designed an undulating ridge-and-furrow pattern, with little rivers of gravel running through to enable access for weeding. The center of the garden is anchored with boxwoods clipped into balls and cones, surrounded by white flowers that begin in spring with early hardy geraniums and end in autumn with asters. Throughout the blooming season, a tapestry of white and green develops with thalictrum, filipendula, asclepia, and *Eryngium yuccifolium*.

Close by is the Terrace Garden, a traditional herbaceous border that was boldly updated with robust, naturalistic perennials and grasses for a lively, untamed look. The palette is mainly pastels, lusciously soft but definitely not pale, peppered with flowers of particularly vibrant hues. The plant heights are fairly similar, creating a billowing sea of texture and color.

In another garden room is a modern Boxwood Garden of repeated concentric circles surrounded by pleached *Tilia cordata*. This garden's design demonstrates that Lady Hopetoun understands the value of simple spaces as well as those that are extravagantly floriferous. She has also created a Beech Walk, Vegetable Garden, Cutting Border, Cottage Knot, and a new arboretum. Because the Walled Garden area is so large, she will undoubtedly create more gardens in the future.

Although the gardens have been an impressive personal success for Lady Hopetoun, she knows that her gardening will not always be a mainly private pleasure. "The deal was that I would start gardening there for my own enjoyment," she mused, "but on the understanding, it would eventually be another asset for the Hopetoun Estate."

A center gravel path with stone borders leads through the Terrace Garden opening into a
circle fringed in a profuse planting of Mexican feather grass (*Nassella tenuissima*).

HOPETOUN HOUSE WALLED GARDEN

Circles of *Persicaria affinis* brighten the garden
in late summer.

FROM TOP The Old Rose Garden is now centered with an irregular circle of boxwood shaped as balls and cones surrounded by white-flowering perennials. • The plantings in the Terrace Garden were planned as a traditional herbaceous border but planted naturalistically with late-season perennials and grasses, all about the same height, in a sumptuous palette of vibrant purples, blues, and pinks.

The Boxwood Garden uses a graphic series of overlapping concentric circles around water basins, framed by a double row of pleached *Tilia cordata*.

The Garden of Cosmic Speculation

HOLYWOOD, DUMFRIESSHIRE

IN A QUIET VALLEY in the Scottish Borders is a garden that one can safely say, without fear of hyperbole, is unique. Covering thirty acres with forty main areas, The Garden of Cosmic Speculation is designed to connect visitors to nature by illustrating the principles of the universe using sculpture and landforms. Its creator, the late Charles Jencks, a landscape designer, cultural theorist, and architectural historian, once said, "What is a garden if not a miniaturization, and celebration, of the place we are in, the universe?" (Yurkewicz 2010).

Born and raised in Baltimore, Jencks spent his life exploring big ideas. In the 1980s, he was one of the first to advocate in his writings and lectures for ornamentation in modern architecture, turning his back on modernism's "less is more" credo in favor of "more is more." Those ideas became known as postmodernism and made him famous. When in the 1990s his interests turned to inquiries into the laws of nature through landscape design, his fame grew.

This thread in his life started almost by accident. He and his late wife, Maggie Keswick, were living at Portrack House, her family's home near the village of Holywood. Because she wanted a place for their children to swim, she had a marshy area dug out to make a lake. The excavated soil accumulated, and after some discussion, Jencks used the soil to build a large landform, sculpted with the double helix structure of DNA in mind, turning a pile of dirt into a stunning mound. It would become a prototype for his approach to creating other features in the garden, and it also suggested a new way for him to design landscapes imbued with symbolism and meaning.

Because of its height, the Snail Mound, the name Jencks chose for that first landform, is the most noticeable earthwork in the garden. Covered in grass, with two paths (the double helix) that spiral upward, it offers views over the garden and into the surrounding sheep pastures. Below are the connected ponds that his wife created, mirror-smooth and gracefully curved. The tail of the snail arcs into one pond to create a narrow peninsula on which one can stand completely surrounded by dark water, and where one can view the mound and ponds from a different perspective.

Nearby is the Snake Mound, a curving 350-foot landform. A series of terraces first twist toward the ponds and then away. In his 2005 book, *The Garden of Cosmic Speculation*, which tells the story of the garden's creation, Jencks wrote, "Curved and counter-curved shapes are structural and often found in nature, for instance in the meander of a river. . . . Waveforms underlie so many natural activities: sea waves, of course, and sand forms left by the incessant waves on the ocean beach; the vortices caused by pulling a solid object through stationary liquid; the swirls of air currents where warm and cold air meet; and the rock curls evident in mountains, a result of a long, slow geological process of movement."

At the Black Hole Terrace, a grid made of synthetic turf and aluminum depicts the warping of space-time near a black hole. The Universe Cascade, a waterfall and white staircase, represent the development of the universe, from the beginning of time to the present. The Quark Walk explores the smallest particle of matter. Throughout the garden, Jencks took every opportunity to create metaphors of the cosmos in gates, walls, sculptures, and plantings; all of these challenge visitors' preconceptions of what a garden is, what it should look like, and what it can mean.

OPPOSITE Gunnera grows along a stream that flows under the bright red Wedge Bridge, which symbolizes the easy way to get to paradise.

The Snake Mound stretches along one of the ponds echoing its curves.

FROM TOP Throughout the garden are beautifully designed and executed details, such as this handsome gate that represents the waves in a soliton, a phenomenon studied by physicists and mathematicians. • Among the sculptures in the garden designed to represent big ideas are these three, from left to right: the Universe, Gaia, and the Atom.

LEFT The Snail Mound, Jencks's first landform, served as a prototype for many others that followed.

Jencks created a warped grid using synthetic turf and aluminum at the Black Hole Terrace
to represent the distortion of space-time caused by a black hole.

Whitburgh House Walled Garden

PATHHEAD, MIDLOTHIAN

SCOTLAND'S BRUTAL JULY WINDS convinced Elizabeth Salvesen that she needed to find a different way to garden. Just as the tallest perennials were about to bloom in her first garden, a traditional English country-style garden, along came the ruthless Scottish gales, and her plants were ravaged. That experience sent her on a wide search, far from her one-acre Walled Garden at Whitburgh House, eleven miles southeast of Edinburgh.

Around 2006, accompanied by her gardener, Vincent Dudley, she began visiting gardens in England and Wales, searching for ideas. They traveled under the tutelage of British garden writer, teacher, and researcher Noel Kingsbury, who took them on a grand tour of European naturalistic gardens. They visited Piet and Anje Oudolf's garden in The Netherlands and the experimental gardens at Hermannshof and Weihenstephan in Germany. Those three gardens, plus the Walled Garden designed by Piet Oudolf at Scampston Hall in North Yorkshire, had the biggest impact on Elizabeth and prompted her to let go of all of her gardening inhibitions and go her own way.

She settled on a formal garden structure with informal plantings—a place to grow vegetables, fruits, and flowers that also welcomed wildlife, that provided year-round interest, and that included contemporary sculptures from the Salvesens' growing collection. The resulting garden that she made, in collaboration with Vincent, shows an impressively bold graphic style and equally bold naturalistic plantings, making it in every way an example of what well-designed twenty-first-century gardens can be.

Today the 200-year-old Walled Garden is divided into rectangular spaces. Visitors enter through a black, wooden double gate and step into a cool space bordered with square-cut beech trees, sometimes called hedges on stilts, and underplanted with *Nepeta* 'Six Hills Giant'. With limited colors and strong shapes, this area provides a restrained antechamber to the rest of the garden, which visitors can view in the space between the tops of the nepeta and the lowest branches of the pruned beech trees.

At the end of the beech rows is a scene with an entirely different feeling. This late-season border includes a zinc sculpture enveloped in feathery *Stipa gigantea* and accented with pots of pale yellow *Argyranthemum* 'Jamaica Primrose'—an example that offers a preview of Elizabeth's Yin and Yang garden style.

To one side is a narrow reflecting pool bordered in substantial limestone coping and surrounded by lawn. Along the edges are closely spaced, oblique apple cordons of old Scottish varieties, their angled stems setting a quiet rhythm. In autumn, red-cheeked apples bring color to an otherwise green garden.

Next to this is a grassy rectangular area bordered by a wide, waist-high hedge. Two arcing lines of *Miscanthus sinensis* 'Flamingo' bend toward each other but do not meet, a graphic demonstration of how to make a spare statement by using lines of a single species. Nearby are raised vegetable beds and a fruit cage that supply fresh produce, an especially satisfying part of the garden for Elizabeth.

On the other side of the entrance allée is a rousing planting combining grasses, biennials, late-season perennials, and clipped shrubs. One first sees a medley of crisp topiary—some rounded, others boxy, and all executed with great confidence. In the middle is a relaxed parterre loosely rimmed with purple-leaved *Prunus cerasifera* 'Pissardii', which is also used to create clean, dense arches at both ends. This sets the color theme for what is planted inside. Castor bean, *Heuchera villosa* 'Palace Purple', and *Brassica oleracea* (Acephala Group) 'Redbor' mingle with persicaria and lythrum. Wheat-colored grasses lighten the scheme alongside white summer phlox, yellow fennel, and lavender-blue catmint. The effect is rich, moody, and sophisticated.

Sited at the back wall is a handsome glasshouse, and beside it are cold frames. For Elizabeth, this is the heart of the garden, where she and Vincent start everything from seeds and cuttings. Nearby is a decked sitting area that seems to be floating on a sea of waving grasses. Dusky purple plants are paired with flashes of orange from nasturtium, *Calendula officinalis* 'Indian Prince', and *Salvia confertiflora*, all enlivened by generous scatterings of Mexican feather grass.

The evenings in late summer and autumn are her favorite times. By then, the garden's grasses and colors are at their peak. The sun is low in the sky, backlighting the garden, and the plantings are luminous.

Molinia caerulea, Anemanthele lessoniana, and *Nassella tenuissima* are accented with pots of hybrid arctotis on each corner of the deck.

A relaxed parterre is bordered in loose purple-leaved *Prunus cerasifera*
'Pissardii', which also forms the arches at the end of the catmint-lined paths.

Orange canna flowers enliven a mixed planting of loosestrife, kniphofia, and verbena.

A custom-made gate near the Walled Garden opens to a path along a meadow that leads to the house.

Scand

inavia

Marianne Folling's Garden

RØNNEDE, ZEALAND, DENMARK

IT TAKES VISION, persistence, and a crusading spirit to be a pioneer for a new kind of gardening in your region, particularly if you stake your livelihood on it. Danish designer Marianne Folling started with a love of perennials and a deep curiosity about the myriad possible combinations of perennials and grasses. Today, she fully embraces naturalistic planting and the wildness that goes with it. In Denmark, this is not only unconventional, but somewhat radical.

Marianne's garden is on the island of Zealand, the largest in Denmark, about fifty miles southwest of Copenhagen and ten miles from the Baltic Sea. The land is flat and continually swept by strong winds, and the soil is sandy. Though winter offers very little sunshine, summer days are gloriously long, with a raking light that makes Marianne's garden glow.

In 1999, she and her husband, Jesper Petersen, moved to the countryside with the intention of creating a larger garden and keeping animals. Near the house was an existing garden, designed in an organic style with shrubs, trees, and a pond. But this garden didn't suit Marianne. She says, "I was strongly inspired by English gardens, especially gardens that had formal elements such as taxus and buxus [hedges and clipped domes] combined with perennials in a more wild and natural style." Instead of removing the existing garden, the couple made a new one the next year out of a one-and-a-half-acre barley field on the property.

Five years later, Marianne indulged a longtime dream and started a retail nursery, where she sold more than 800 perennial varieties. She immersed herself in propagation and growing. It was an exciting time that enabled her to take her knowledge of perennials to a new level, but the venture did not last. She closed the nursery after seven years and turned to designing gardens, giving lectures, teaching courses, writing magazine articles, and further developing her garden, all in the service of spreading the word about perennials.

By this time, Piet Oudolf's work with grasses and naturalistic plantings was becoming better known. Marianne saw her chance to create a garden in the Oudolf style, when she and her husband added a modern wooden deck on the sunniest side of the house. After removing the original garden around the deck, she planted a new garden, where grasses such as Calamagrostis ×acutiflora 'Overdam', Leymus arenarius 'Blue Dune', and Stipa calamagrostis take center stage starting in August. Animated and feathery, these grasses bring an effervescent end to the gardening season.

The former barley fields are now surrounded by mature windbreaks and narrow slat fences to keep animals out. Visitors enter this part of the garden through the White Allée, with a generous corridor of Laburnum ×watereri 'Vossii', underplanted with Annabelle hydrangeas, white persicarias, white-edged hostas, alliums, and clipped boxwood. It is always lovely here, and Marianne's design has made sure of that, but in June when the twelve laburnums produce long clusters of pealike flowers, the allée is breathtaking, with wave after wave of cascading branches and fragrant, lemon-yellow blossoms. For Marianne, the allée is her greatest success.

OPPOSITE The Perennial Garden, enclosed by beech hedges, offers a place to rest and enjoy the lightness and dynamism of ornamental grasses and perennials.

FROM TOP A mix of liatris, salvia, echinops, stipa, perovskia, eupatorium, sesleria, agastache, and angelica demonstrate Marianne's naturalistic planting style. • Marianne likes to use perennials in abundance and prefers carefully planned color schemes.

In the White Allée, laburnums are underplanted with
allium, thalictrum, sedge, and corydalis.

A gazebo made from rustic rebar adds a graceful profile on
a misty morning in the Perennial Garden.

Peter Korn's Garden

LANDVETTER, VÄSTRA GÖTALAND, SWEDEN

WHAT FASCINATES PETER KORN about growing plants goes beyond their beauty or rarity. In his garden, he actually creates habitats to provide plants with environments that closely match their wild homes. If his garden doesn't include a particular plant's natural habitat, he gets out his shovel and creates it, even if it takes enormous effort and a very long time. "I don't limit myself," he explains. "If it's necessary to dig for years and move thousands of tons of material by hand to create the landscape, I do it."

Peter's garden is located about a half hour southeast of Gothenburg, only sixteen miles from the sea. When he moved to the property, an eighty-year-old dense reforestation of spruce dominated the land and the soils were poor and thin. He had become interested in gardening only a few years earlier, and his first attempts at growing in this new place were less than successful, with few plants surviving the wet winters. After learning a hard lesson in the importance of habitat, in 2002, he began removing the spruce and started gardening with relentless determination to discover what plants want.

Visitors arrive on a wooded lane that opens up to a five-acre garden with a rolling topography scooped out of the forest. On one side, hugging the perimeter trees, is an old log house, with a greenhouse farther on. The rest of the garden is filled with large, asymmetrical planting beds, many with rugged rock outcrops and stony surfaces, with dramatic, craggy cliffs in the back. Soft lawn paths flow between the organically shaped beds in some parts of the garden, with paths paved in gritty aggregate in others.

"I'm not a collector," Peter explains, "but I can't resist new plants." Each year he sites his new finds in beds he has created specifically to provide environments that mimic as close as possible their wild habit. Each crest and hollow, every cavity and mound, provides a different microclimate in which thousands of species can thrive. Steppe, desert, alpine, prairie, forest—they are all in this garden. It gives new meaning to the term "naturalistic."

In one part of the garden, the original flora still exists. In the far corner, opposite the log house, is an area Peter calls the heart of his garden—a natural marsh fed by a spring that he discovered while excavating the cliffs. He added a wooden footbridge over the dark water, which mirrors the sky. Frogs thrive here among the rocks and old tree stumps, surrounded by haircap moss and native heather.

In the winter, when many of the plants are not visible, the garden looks like a raw moonscape, with barren boulders, vertical rock faces, and loose scree surrounded by dark, angular spruce trees. During the summer, the immense, rugged garden bursts into bloom, and the network of meandering paths takes visitors past created habitats that include alpine meadows, mountain tops, flowering meadows, forest glades, and even wet jungles.

In about half of his garden, Peter forgoes enriching beds with compost and instead grows plants in up to fifteen inches of sand. By trial and error, he has learned that sand is more stable than soil. "The disadvantage of mixtures containing any kind of compost is that they decompose. After a year or two, all that is left is some rather sticky topsoil, no matter how fluffy it was to begin with" (Korn 2008). Sand, however, is free-draining, reducing the chance that plants will rot in wet, cold winters. And in summer, when the surface of the sand can be hot and dry, most weed seeds burn off, while plant roots at the lower layers stay cool and damp.

Peter has learned that plants growing in sand develop deeper, wider root systems in order to survive. They produce more compact, stronger growth that doesn't have to be staked, and they withstand drought much better than plants in soil. When Peter gets a new plant, he washes all the soil off the roots before planting it in the sand, immediately introducing the plant to a trial by fire.

Making this garden has been a herculean undertaking. And the effort required to give plants what they want is not easily understood. Peter says the most frequent question he hears from visitors is "Was it a quarry?"

OPPOSITE *Ramonda myconi*, the Pyrenean violet, grows in the shady crevices of a moist stone wall with mosses and ferns.

Next to the massive rock garden, Peter sits in the heart of
his garden beside a natural bog.

CLOCKWISE FROM TOP LEFT *Stipa pulcherrima* has long, feathery awns so light that they seem to be in motion. • Blooming in early spring, a silky-haired pasque flower is tucked in next to a boulder in one of Peter's scree beds. • *Gentiana acaulis* blooms in a shade of deep blue that is rarely seen in gardens.• *Phlox kelseyi*, native to southern Idaho, brings early spring color to Peter's garden.

Flowers enliven a slope in the naturalistically designed
rock garden.

Germ

any

Garten Moorriem

ELSFLETH, WESERMARSCH, LOWER SAXONY

AFTER YEARS OF VISITING GARDENS throughout Europe, a walk through Piet Oudolf's garden in Hummelo, Netherlands, in the late 1990s helped Ute and Albrecht Ziburski realize how powerful perennials can be in creating special garden atmospheres. The idea of forming emotional connections with others through planting resonated so deeply that they began searching for a distinctive place to make a garden. In 2006, they settled on a property near the village of Moorriem in Northern Germany.

Garten Moorriem is situated on flat, fertile marshland that was drained by the Dutch in the Middle Ages. The ancient cultural landscape is preserved today in long, narrow properties and half-timber farmhouses with low, thatched roofs. In the eighteenth and nineteenth centuries, lush flower gardens became popular in these village homes, where they served as examples of prestige. These gardens developed into an important part of the local culture that persists to this day.

For the new garden behind the Ziburskis' farmhouse, the couple had everything decided before the first shovel dug into the ground. Together, they designed the overall layout, while Ute, who has a talent for making harmonious plant combinations, created the planting plan. In 2007, with the master plan in hand, they built the one-and-a-half-acre garden themselves.

Visitors enter the garden through a gate in a white picket fence beside the tall, gabled house and proceed down a rustic path made of patinated brick recycled from an old road. Feathery *Nassella tenuissima* is planted between cobbles along the home's foundation, interrupted by a collection of brightly colored, potted pelargoniums.

A lawn stretches out at the back of the house, accented by a few fruit trees and four low topiary balls arranged along an axis that aligns with the peak of the house roof. Ahead, at either side of the axis, the Ziburskis have created rectangular perennial beds bordered by hedges and lawn, an interpretation of a traditional rural garden typical of this area. Here, larkspurs, cranesbills, and peonies bloom in early summer, and dahlias, crocosmias, annual zinnias, phlox, and asters provide late-summer color.

Crossing a bridge over an ancient drainage ditch shaded by a tall oak, visitors step from the historical and traditional into the contemporary and naturalistic. Here, the Ziburskis have made a garden with a powerful and special atmosphere that emotionally engages its visitors. A long lawn stretches forward, opening to a farm meadow at the far end. On either side, deep, color-themed, curvaceous borders are filled with rich compositions of densely planted perennials and grasses. The planting on the left side includes a fiery mix of helenium, goldenrod, cone flowers, and dahlias. Narrow inner paths encourage exploration, bringing visitors face-to-face with the saturated hues.

The 130-foot border on the opposite side of the lawn is the highlight of the garden. Planted predominantly with long-blooming *Echinacea purpurea*, the bed is a cool, dreamy blend of many shades of purples and pinks. Monarda, aster, and phlox mingle with the purple coneflowers, along with sanguisorba, agastache, and thalictrum. A few creamy white selenium, calamintha, and artemisia lighten the palette. *Cornus controversa* 'Variegata' anchors the bed, while solemn yew columns lead the eye along the internal, curving lawn path. Most striking of all is the scattering of statuesque *Angelica gigas*, with dark merlot–colored umbels hovering above the perennial array.

In these borders, the Ziburskis practice "creative weeding," a term coined in the 1990s by Dutch gardener and artist Ton ter Linden. Each spring, this involves close, ground-level scrutiny of every seedling to determine which will stay and which will be discarded. "The effort we put into these natural flowerbeds is quite high," explains Albrecht. "But this work is necessary so that the aesthetic balance of a garden, at least according to our ideas, is maintained . . . over the whole summer."

In early mornings, when the garden is enshrouded in mist and the sunlight filters through the trees, the perennial borders are spectacular. They impart a serene illusion of naturalness, a garden atmosphere well made.

OPPOSITE A grass path makes a beautiful sweeping curve, taking visitors into the middle of the echinacea planting.

FROM TOP A soft, colorful border is planted in calamint, thalictrum, veronicastrum, and *Doellingeria umbellate*, along with a few echinaceas. • In winter, following a frost, echinacea seedheads and plant skeletons paint a subtle scene.

LEFT The echinacea borders on a misty morning are punctuated with dark yew columns. *Cornus controversa* 'Variegata' gracefully anchors the middle of the borders.

Bathed in early morning light, *Helenium* 'Wyndley' and *H.* 'Waltraut' bloom in the hot border alongside *Rudbeckia laciniata* and *Calamagrostis ×acutiflora* 'Karl Foerster'.

HORTVS

HILDEN, NORTH RHINE-WESTPHALIA

BESIDE A BUSTLING STREET in Hilden, Germany, a stylish garden flanked by mature woodland surrounds a house. This calm oasis amid the urban clatter, HORTVS, belongs to the gifted garden designer Peter Janke and his husband, landscape architect Michael Frinke.

Peter started the garden in 2006 by building a strong structure with some formal aspects and filling it with wildlife-friendly, naturalistic plantings. "I love to see how these two different design ideas play together during the seasons," he says. "In the winter, my garden shows its formal bones very clearly, while dried grasses and seedheads catch the winter sun. In summer, you can hardly see the formality of hedges, paths, and clipped evergreens when thousands of lush, herbaceous plants and grasses create a softening layer."

Visitors to the three-and-a-half-acre site are enraptured. One person told Peter, "If I knew that heaven would look like your garden, I would seriously try to become a better person." They enter HORTVS via a driveway that bisects the front garden. Bordered by a boxwood-edged allée of slender, perfectly spaced *Cupressus sempervirens* enhanced with a frothy underplanting of *Gaura lindheimeri* 'Whirling Butterflies', this processional entrance garden hints at what is to come. It also announces subtly that a key to understanding HORTVS is its structure: axis and cross axis, allées and focal points, geometric enclosures, and organically shaped open spaces.

To the left of the driveway, behind a planting of naturally statuesque shrubs, is a Gravel Garden, an homage to Peter's mentor, the late Beth Chatto, the eminent English plantsman and garden designer. At a crucial point in his development as a designer, Peter worked in Chatto's Essex garden and came away with a profound commitment to an ecologically astute style of planting that she called "right plant, right place."

For the Gravel Garden, Peter chose the windiest, hottest part of his property, which also had free draining, gritty soil. He filled it with a broad mix of perennials and grasses, accented by trees and shrubs that not only tolerate but thrive in these conditions. An irregular path flows around two oval islands—one large, the other small—that serve as microcosms of the plantings all around the perimeter. A single *Juniperus scopulorum* 'Blue Arrow' anchors the smaller island, contrasting beautifully with broad-leaved *Acanthus hungaricus*, gossamer *Nassella tenuissima*, and erect *Iris* 'Pearly Dawn'. At ground level are *Aster ericoides* f. *prostratus* 'Snow Flurry', *Oxalis adenophylla*, and *Acaena inermis* 'Purpurea'. The islands provide small-scale demonstrations of Peter's lively naturalistic planting style, each a tutorial on how to create layered plantings.

Deep in the corner, opposite the Gravel Garden, is the Woodland Garden. Here, in the cool shade of ancient oak, beech, and hornbeam, the atmosphere is damp and quiet. A mulch path curves along a bog. This is where Peter indulges his love of mosses and ferns and made a home for large-leaved *Darmera peltata*, *Hosta* 'Sun Power', and *Rodgersia aesculifolia*. Plantings of Hakone grass (*Hakonechloa* spp.) and sedge (*Carex* spp.) are scattered about, along with primula, asarum, and epimedium. Farther down the path, under an arching tree branch, is a rusty classic urn featuring an elegant eternal flame.

Peter's preferred circular route includes a Silver Garden and a Meadow, both circular in form. A lush Perennial Garden has deep beds facing a large, meandering lawn and backed by the woodland. At the end of the walk is a square Herb Garden, bursting with wildish plantings and recently enclosed with a handsome, chest-high, weathering steel wall. The nursery managed by Michael is to one side.

What makes the couple most happy now that HORTVS is reaching maturity is that even though the garden is bordered by a busy street in the middle of a city, Peter's emphasis on diverse plantings has brought wildlife to the garden, which now supports bees, birds, and bats. It has become a place of tranquility in harmony with nature, a refuge in a stressful world.

OPPOSITE In the fall, colorful deciduous shrubs glow and grasses become even more gossamer, with tall evergreen cypress in the background.

In spring, hundreds of daffodils bloom in the circular Meadow.

A cobblestone path leads through the Silver Garden, framed by fast-growing
Salix alba 'Liempde', which are pruned annually to keep them narrow.

FROM TOP The lawn meanders along richly planted perennial borders, leading to a small bosque of birch trees. • Elegant inflorescences of *Stipa gigantea* catch the morning light surrounded by white-flowering *Salvia sclarea* and *Eschscholzia californica*.

Peter Berg's Garden

SINZIG-WESTUM, AHRWEILER, RHINELAND-PALATINATE

AS A CHILD, Peter Berg spent much of his time outside in the terraced hillside vineyards near his home in the Eifel region of western Germany. These steep slopes, terraced with dry stone walls, left an impression on Peter, and many years later, his intimate familiarity with stone and precipitous topography informs much about the way he makes gardens.

After earning a degree and working as a civil engineer, he retrained as a gardener in his late twenties. During an extended, personally imposed apprenticeship, he gained practical experience in as many horticultural and landscaping skills as possible, traveling to Ireland and Japan for workshops and mentoring. In 2000, he founded GartenLandschaft Berg & Co. with his business partner, Susanne Förster. The firm specializes in a style that tames slopes into modern spaces through expert handling of stone.

Peter's own garden is in Sinzig-Westum, a small town located above the Rhine River in an area characterized by fir forests, rugged rock formations, and vineyards. His narrow slice of land is perched on a steep, south-facing slope that rises more than 130 feet from the street to the back property line. When he arrived in 1985, the slope had been used for growing grapes, with meadows and the occasional fruit tree. Since then, he has built seven terraced spaces, connected by one hundred stone steps carved from the slope, and retained by dry stone walls, blocks, boulders, and slabs in every configuration imaginable. One terrace is for dining, another for growing vegetables, and another for a vineyard. A Rockery offers views of a meadow, and at the highest point is a modern swinging bench suspended from a tree, which floats above it all.

His latest experiment, in 2018, was a pavilion nestled against the hillside on the fifth terrace. The structure, created from large, prefabricated, board-formed concrete elements, stylistically refers to the Bauhaus, the avant-garde movement of classic modern style that developed in Germany in the first half of the twentieth century. It was the biggest construction challenge he and his crew had ever faced, requiring all of their expertise and ingenuity to complete. Glass extends from ceiling to floor on two sides of the slate-gray pavilion, which has a planted green roof.

Next to the pavilion is an impressive waterfall built of craned-in basalt boulders, rugged and craggy with sandy-beige and rust-colored surfaces. The repetition of sharp vertical edges both unifies and enlivens, lightening the bulky assemblage, with water pouring over the stones into a pond edged in dark green, tubular stems of equisetum. To the left of the waterfall, Peter carved out a nook with huge retaining blocks of basalt, furnished with a small table and chairs. This terrace design juxtaposes intimacy and openness, intensity and calm, manmade and natural. He considers this the heart of his garden.

Peter uses soft plants as a foil to the heavy stone in his terraces. In his 2018 book, *Nature. Aesthetics. Design.*, he writes, "The incredible variety of greens in plants perfectly complements the stone structures in my gardens. They soften the stones' dominance and subtly ground them." In the pockets between stones, he first plants trees, with his favorites being *Quercus pubescens* and *Q. robur* (Fastigiata Group). The understory layer comes next, with *Cercis siliquastrum*, *Cornus kousa*, and *Pyrus* species. The final layer includes grasses, which inject movement into the garden, and perennials, always in hues of blue, gray, or white because the colors of the sky suggest quietness and tranquility.

It takes determination and endurance to create a garden that involves such heavy elements on sloping landscapes, but to Peter, the importance of expressing the character of the region overrides the difficulties he encounters. The *genius loci*—the pervading spirit of a place—directs his designs and his life's work.

A color palette of blue-purple, gray, and white adds a quiet calmness to the garden spaces.

The Glasshouse Terrace, with its Bauhaus-inspired pavilion and beautifully crafted, rugged waterfall, is Peter's favorite part of the garden.

FROM TOP Salvias, ferns, and evergreen shrubs—some natural, others shaped—grow in planting pockets to soften the boulders and slabs. • The Wine Terrace overlooks the surrounding countryside.

Antique basalt blocks border a lounging nook in the Rockery,
surrounded by umbrella-shaped mulberry trees.

De Terptuin

MANTGUM, FRIESLAND

IF YOU'RE DRIVING through the tiny village of Mantgum, fifteen miles from the North Sea, it would be impossible not to notice the small garden next to the old church. The space is dominated by eleven hornbeams, clipped into slender ten-foot columns. In spring, their new growth complements the brick on the double-gabled cottage with mustard-colored trim and teal-colored doors. A combination of fennel, persicaria, selinum, fuchsia, and wiry verbena engulf each column and cascade through the iron fence. The overall effect is energetic, bold, and modern.

This small front garden with a big personality belongs to garden designer Nico Kloppenborg, who used the nineteenth-century church consistory as a studio for his design practice in the 1990s, and some years later began the garden with a colleague. In 2005, he made the building his home and started developing the garden further. He named the garden De Terptuin, Dutch for mound garden, which is a reference to the ancient practice, before there were dikes, of building clay mounds, or terps, in the Dutch lowlands to provide safe ground during seasonal flooding. The village of Mantgum was built on such a mound above the surrounding fields.

Visitors enter De Terptuin on a brick path surrounded by more hornbeam columns and perennials. Within a few steps, one arrives at the pocket-sized entry to the gravel path leading to the front door, where fatsia grows within the gravel and two wooden tubs are planted with nassella. The plants on this side of the front garden include *Helleborus orientalis*, *Rosa* 'Nevada', *Thalictrum* 'Elin', and graceful mounds of *Hakonechloa macra* 'Aureola'. At the far end in a quiet corner sits an antique Buddha.

The brick path continues alongside the house, making a sharp right turn at its back corner, revealing three hornbeams shaped to lean into the house wall, perhaps a nod to the buttresses on the church next door. At their feet, Nico planted *Euphorbia characias* subsp. *wulfenii,* its chartreuse flowers exploding against narrow, blue-green leaves.

From here the garden falls off abruptly nearly fifteen feet, the result of a farmer in the early twentieth-century selling off some fertile terp soil to build a tennis court. Inspired by Asian tea plantations and Italian Renaissance garden stairways, Nico devised a ramping path with hairpin turns. The path is paved in recycled broken slate tiles from a former church roof and edged in rusty steel. Hornbeam hedges frame the path in gradually sloping heights, sometimes rising in relation to the path, other times descending. The walk down the path is a slightly disorienting journey, reminding one of walking through a maze.

At the bottom of the path, the tennis court has given way to a pleasant rectangular garden room, a place to breathe and relax after the bemusing walk down. The room is enclosed by a hornbeam hedge, pruned to a shallow, scalloped top, extending from corner to corner. Planted in the recycled slate paving are a smattering of ornamental grasses, perennials, and shrubs. Fifteen years ago in the middle of this space, Nico planted twelve birches in a tight cluster; they now form what he calls "a beautiful tree bouquet." Turning to look up to the house, one sees the hedges crisscrossing the slope in a sculptural zigzag pattern. In this quite small garden, Nico has made an energetic, bold, and modern statement.

A Buddha sculpture rests in a quiet corner of the front garden.

OPPOSITE A bold planting of selinum, persicaria, crocosmia, and fennel greets visitors at the sidewalk.

The inner front garden is framed by clipped hornbeam columns.

FROM TOP A small, casual dining terrace is positioned next to the house, with a wooden table and mustard-colored stools. • Persicaria dominates the beds surrounding the brick path between the front and back gardens.

Hornbeam hedges crisscross the slope, framing the ramping path that leads to the lowest area of the garden.

Jakobstuin

JISTRUM, FRIESLAND

FOR JAAP DE VRIES, plants are not the most important part of his garden; instead, it is the atmosphere, the elusive quality that is nearly impossible to put into words. "It is something you experience," he says. "Sometimes it is the light, sometimes the wind, [and sometimes] the mist." These uncontrollable natural elements create moments in his garden that are compelling and memorable.

In the 1990s, as a new gardener, Jaap was drawn to The Dutch Wave, a style of naturalistic planting developed by Piet Oudolf, Ton ter Linden, and the late Henk Gerritsen, that combines strong perennials (with no deadheading, dividing, or staking) with ornamental grasses using an artful approach that mimics the way plants grow in the wild. After visits to Hermannshof, a botanical garden in Weinheim, Germany, to see the planting designs of its director Cassian Schmidt, Jaap was smitten. In 2005, he quit his job as a theater technician and became a full-time gardener.

In 2007, he and his partner, Maria van de Molen, purchased Jakobstuin, near the small farm village of Jistrum in the Dutch province of Friesland, about twenty miles from the North Sea. They bought the property with the specific intent of making a garden there. Jaap had worked out some basic design principles he intended to use: the garden would have an open character with no hedges, trees, or other obstacles to block views. He wanted to be able to walk through the plantings—not just stand in front of them as in a traditional garden. His design would allow views from one area to another. He also intended for this garden to convey a soft naturalness through the use of lots of grasses.

Several years after moving to the property, Jaap chose the three-quarter-acre sheep pasture in front of the house to make his garden. He had no plans on paper and started by simply mowing a sinuous central path aligned with the living room window. Then he mowed secondary paths until there were eight planting beds. Then, tapping into a well of courage with the resolve to do things his own way, he started planting.

Ten years later, Jaap thinks of his garden as a perennial meadow. Existing alder, beech, hawthorn, and oak trees frame the rectangular garden on two sides, while the other two sides are planted with statuesque *Aralia californica*, *Eupatorium maculatum* (Atropurpureum Group) 'Purple Bush', and *Persicaria amplexicaulis* 'Firetail'. Within the border planting, a rustic wooden bench and chairs offer places to pause and take pleasure in the sumptuous display.

Walking along the grass paths through perennials, grasses, and annuals in late summer, one is struck by the lightness and airiness of these plantings. Purple coneflowers, cleomes, and *Verbena bonariensis* dance amid wafting drifts of *Nassella tenuissima* in one bed, while in another, the delicate grass scampers among rusty Gloriosa daisies and chartreuse *Solidago rugosa* 'Loydser Crown'. "I think using *Nassella tenuissima* was my biggest success," remarks Jaap. "It gives the garden its special feel."

Among the 10,000 perennials and grasses planted at Jakobstuin, Jaap has some seasonal favorites, whose colors and forms are particularly appealing. In spring, the pairing of *Amsonia tabernaemontana* var. *salicifolia* and *Euphorbia griffithii* 'Fireglow' attracts his eye. In the summer, *Helenium* 'Luc' with *Liatris pycnostachya* stand out. And in autumn, he savors the ball-shaped flowers of *Aralia californica*, which share the coppery hues of the feathery plumes of *Miscanthus sinensis* 'Malepartus'.

Every day during the growing season, he sets up his tripod to photograph areas that are particularly beautiful and shares his photos on social media. His favorite images feature the special morning light and the golden moments at the end of the day. The atmosphere he captures in these images draws hundreds to his photography, and faithful followers from around the world visit the garden each year. He enjoys sharing his knowledge about plants and gardening, and he learns from his visitors as well, whose reactions to Jakobstuin are often deeply moving. "I never knew that a garden could be such an emotional thing," he says. "I sometimes have people in the garden that start crying. That has a big effect on me."

Frequently, visitors ask how they can create a garden such as his. "Just do it," he replies. "Don't be afraid to make a mistake. You can always change the things you don't like."

The fountain-like habit of *Ammophila breviligulata* adds a
graceful note to the summer garden.

FROM TOP Jaap provides places for visitors to sit and take in the abundant and varied planting. • Pennisetum, amsonia, and *Eupatorium maculatum* (Atropurpureum Group) 'Phantom' create a soft, natural margin along the central grass path that extends to the end of the perennial meadow.

Lianne's Siergrassen

DE WILP, GRONINGEN

AS WINDS FROM THE NORTH SEA blow unchecked across the flat fields of the Northern Netherlands, they eventually arrive at Lianne Pot's prairie garden near De Wilp where they rustle through the grasses and perennials in waves. The garden is animated with a soft yet energized atmosphere.

Lianne's garden-making journey began when she spotted ornamental grasses while searching for plants to add to her first garden, after moving to the countryside in 1995. "I discovered that grasses have many different structures, different forms, and so many possibilities in usage that I wanted to collect them all. I did not see them in [other] gardens and wondered, why not?" As her fascination with grasses continued to grow, she enrolled in a garden design and construction course. Then she opened her own garden design business, started a nursery, created her first demonstration garden, and, in 2005, became the holder of the Dutch collection of Poaceae, part of the National Plant Collections scheme that aims to conserve the diversity of garden plants.

Her interest in prairies was awakened after she encountered prairie grasses, whose dense roots grow deeply, seeking moisture and nutrients. To learn more about them, she visited German prairie gardens, and within a few years, she traveled to the United States to explore the few remaining true prairies there. "In Wyoming, South Dakota, Nebraska, and Missouri, I saw echinacea in the wild for the first time," she says. "It was amazing to see them in their natural habitat!" She was also awed by wild-growing *Hystrix patula*, *Sorghastrum nutans*, *Andropogon gerardii*, achillea, rudbeckia, rose, monarda, helenium, liatris, eryngium, and bouteloua. "Eventually I got so excited that I wanted to make my own prairie garden in the Netherlands!"

The spacious prairie garden she made is situated behind her thatch-roofed farmhouse on a quiet country road. A bit larger than an acre in size, the garden is completely open to the sky and filled with a rich, interwoven array of nearly 12,000 densely planted grasses and perennials. Using the venation pattern of an oak leaf as a guide, Lianne laid out a curving gravel path system that leads visitors into the middle of the plantings. She hopes the garden is immersive and offers an intimate, sensual experience. On the path loop farthest from the house is a viewing mound that rises more than eight feet above the rest of the garden. There, visitors are offered an impressive panorama overlooking the entire garden.

Lianne has come to think of her prairie garden as an artificial ecosystem of designed plant communities, dynamic and colorful, with repetition and movement. It resembles nature more closely than most gardens and works with natural processes. "My goal is not to make an exact copy of the prairie, but to design beautiful, durable, long-living plant communities that do not need to be fertilized or irrigated and in which a minimum of weeds arise."

In February or March, everything is cut down, and the chopped material is removed. Then Lianne weeds thoroughly, sometimes with help from family members or volunteers. There are fewer weeds than one might expect here, because the plants are spaced closely (about thirteen to seventeen inches on center) and weeds are shaded out. Some perennials self-seed, but three inches of lava rock mulch ensure that self-seeding is reduced.

Morning is her favorite time in the garden, especially in August and September, when the grasses are spectacular and many flowers are still in bloom. The colors of the plants are warmer and so is the light. "There is so much energy," she says. "You see the different textures, forms, and structures of the plantings, the repetitions, the feeling. It's a very special kind of atmosphere and the morning is so promising and fresh."

OPPOSITE *Calamagrostis brachytricha* sends up fluffy plumes in early autumn, intermingled with colorful *Solidago rigida*, verbena, and echinacea.

Liatris seedheads mingle with *Imperata cylindrica* 'Red Baron'.

LEFT Airy buff-colored grasses, including deschampsia, calamagrostis, and stipa, dominate parts of the garden.

In autumn, russet-colored *Miscanthus sinensis* takes center stage and sets off the blond coloration of *Pennisetum massaicum* 'Red Bunny Tails'.

Gravel paths wind through the prairie-style planting, immersing visitors in a rich diversity of plants.

The Stream Garden

WASPIK, NOORD-BRABANT

WHEN JOHN AND GERDA REKKERS contacted garden designer Noël van Mierlo in the summer of 2015, they knew the kind of garden they wanted. It was to be a natural, peaceful place with curving lines that would harmoniously blend into their one-acre property. Trees and terraces would be located in the sun as well as in the shade, and the garden would be welcoming to visitors, birds, and insects. Perhaps the most essential item on their garden wish list was a sense of privacy; they lived on the property alongside their business, a busy marina on a branch of the Meuse River, and the time had come for a bit of separation.

When Noël, a winner of design awards in both the Netherlands and Great Britain, heard the couple's requests, he picked up on something more. The landscapes they loved and described were the places they had visited in the Alps, while hiking along boulder-strewn streams that were different in every way from the low, flat, and rockless topography of the polder where they lived. Noël realized that the couple's garden would need to be a place to escape from the challenges of work—it would require an aura of vacation and adventure.

The following year, he built a garden centered on a naturalistic pond with river-sourced water, situated next to the house terrace. Flowing from the pond is a 325-foot meandering stream, scattered with boulders and rocks imported from Luxembourg since the Netherlands has no rocks. A gentle current drops into small waterfalls, before it eventually reaches a larger pond at the far side of the property. Along the stream is a rustic, linear boardwalk with uneven edges, built from wood recycled from an old boat deck. Noël thinks of this as the heart of the garden: "It really is the magnet that gets you out of your chair to start exploring."

A log wall now forms a visual, and psychological, barrier that separates the garden from the marina. Stout, square, wooden bollards, originally used in the marina, gently separate public space from private. Two terraces, one in the shade of an existing tree and the other opposite on the sunny pond edge, are paved with small, square-cut sandstone. Paths made from tiny, flat rocks and well-compacted sand lead around the pond through flourishing plantings of calamintha, ceratostigma, and tiarella, along with sedum, helenium, rudbeckia, anemone, and oakleaf hydrangea. Near the pond edge are royal fern, rodgersia, and astilbe, and in the water margins pickerelweed thrives with the delicate Dutch native flowering rush, adding a light, airy touch.

Though only a few years old, this naturalistic garden looks settled and well established, as does the pond, which is full of life and home to frogs, fish, and ducks. Trees and perennials are host to birds, bees, and butterflies. This garden provides the Rekkers with the privacy they longed for. "It is a luxury to have our own small park," says Gerda, "and be able to stay at home and still enjoy a natural environment."

Morning is the best part of each day for the Rekkers. The garden faces east, and as the sun rises, the effect over the pond and stream is breathtaking. In October, when the sun is less glaring and the light seems filled with a golden dust, the garden glows.

OPPOSITE Helenium, rudbeckia, and agastache brighten the path leading to the boardwalk.

Watching the sun rise over the garden is a favorite daily
experience for the Rekkers.

Astilbes grow near the pond edge and in the water margins pickerelweed thrives in large clumps.

A sitting area overlooks the pond, where pickerelweed and water lilies bloom.

Belgi

Country Garden

NEAR YPRES, WEST FLANDERS

FROM THE BEGINNING, Hein and Veronique Vandecasteele-Hostens wanted a simple garden that blended into the surrounding landscape—a place where they could enjoy the beauty of the countryside in peace and quiet. When asked what inspired them, Veronique replied, "Less is more."

They had moved to a twelve-acre property in West Flanders, less than eight miles from the French border, nestled amid agricultural land, with gentle hills and occasional dark woods. They were not happy with the existing garden, however, which they believed was not in harmony with its surroundings. For three years, they removed all the elements they found unpleasant; with those distractions gone, only a few weeping willows remained. In 2001, after they sowed grass seed to improve the view all around, they contacted landscape architect Andy Malengier, who is known for creating quiet outdoor spaces with a pared-down aesthetic.

Andy set out to design a garden that would contribute to the quality of life that the couple required and that would enable the house and the garden to be in harmony with the bucolic countryside. "Creating the opportunity for the owners to be able to enjoy the surrounding landscape on a daily basis was a very important basic principle for me," he says.

There were other concerns to address as well. Andy wanted the garden to be a combination of open and sheltered areas, with some spaces looking inward and others looking outward. And it had to be a functional garden that provided views of the countryside while maintaining the family's privacy. Issues of wind and water also needed to be dealt with—not to mention the heliport that Hein wanted to include.

Built in two phases, and finished in 2011, the formal and spare garden was created with no superfluous elements. In the front about thirty feet from the road is a tall beech hedge, and a handsome driveway of Belgian porphyry cobbles leads to the house, where terraces paved in Chinese granite tiles are bordered by rounded yew hedges. The dining terrace is shaded by three weeping willows, their descending branches trimmed level. A wooded area of mainly spruce serves as a windbreak on the opposite side of the driveway, but on the other side of the house and in the back, views are open to pastures with grazing cows and sheep, and paddling ducks that float in a natural pond next to the helipad. In the distance, rising over the horizon, is the village church steeple. A ha-ha prevents animals from wandering into the garden.

To design a garden with the idea of "less is more" is to use basic elements, to include only what is essential, to offer access to the beauty that is right in front of you. "Our garden is a peaceful place where we can quietly enjoy the beauty of nature," says Veronique. "It feels like it has always been like this."

OPPOSITE The ha-ha allows uninterrupted views to the countryside, including cows and sheep grazing in a pasture.

FROM TOP Hoarfrost bathes the garden and fields in silver. • The sun shining behind a mass planting of miscanthus illuminates its fine texture next to one of the buildings. • The dining terrace is sheltered by the original weeping willows and surrounded by yew hedges.

The ha-ha separates the couple's garden from surrounding fields to keep grazing animals away.

Dina Deferme's Garden

HASSELT, LIMBURG

"FROM WHEN I WAS A LITTLE GIRL," says Dina Deferme, "I always came home in summer with flowers in my hands." This passion was encouraged by her grandmother, who was an accomplished gardener. In Dina's memory, she was always working in her flower beds. The apple didn't fall far from the tree.

As a teenager, Dina decided that she would devote her life to horticulture, and in 1988, she earned a degree in landscape architecture from Ghent University. After traveling to England to visit gardens there, she became interested in the work of Gertrude Jekyll, the early-twentieth-century British horticulturist, garden designer, writer, and artist, whose design methods continue to inspire many today. She was especially influenced by Jekyll's famous gardens at Hestercombe House, Munstead Wood, and the Manor House at Upton Grey. Dina's design style was evolving toward an English style, with overflowing flowers within a strong structure.

In the early 1990s, Dina and her husband, Tony Pirrote, a landscape contractor, purchased a property in the countryside in the Flanders region of northern Belgium. Here the summers are cool, the winters are mild, and the soil is sandy. Almost immediately, she drew up a garden plan, and piece-by-piece, Tony built a nearly four-acre garden around their farmhouse.

"The garden has to have a good structure," says Dina. "It has to radiate peace, has to be in balance, has to look natural, and must be interesting and magnificent during the whole season." She applied this philosophy to designing her garden by creating distinct areas, most separated by tall hedges. She also included her signature floriferous borders everywhere.

The Entrance Garden is the epitome of a front country garden, with a broad lawn, shade trees, and colorful multiseasonal plantings. The Shade Garden's circular terrace offers a cool place to relax on a warm summer day. Herbs and vegetables grow among curving boxwood hedges in the Herb Garden. A lofty, vine-covered iron pergola crowns the Yellow and Blue Garden. A handsome perennial-faced hedge encircles the Tea Garden, where visitors can rest and refresh, and at sunset, the Evening Terrace is the place to be. Dina's horses and chickens have the run of two large meadows.

At the heart of the garden is the Courtyard, which is enclosed on three sides by white stucco buildings with olive-green doors and shutters. Granite sett paths lead to a central, circular patio bordered in a square-cut boxwood hedge. "I never lay patios directly against the house," says Dina. "It is much more pleasant to sit on a patio that is completely surrounded by plants and fragrant flowers." She has placed vintage white furniture here and covers the table with a tablecloth, which suggests the importance of this space to her. Flowers are all around—in the borders, climbing up walls, and in pots—with *Rosa* 'Petite Lisette', *Eupatorium maculatum* (Atropurpureum Group), *Strobilanthes attenuata*, *Veronicastrum virginicum* f. *roseum* 'Pink Glow', *Phlox paniculata* 'Blue Boy', and *Hosta* 'Royal Standard'. The color palette is soft and the atmosphere is charming and cozy.

A garden area on one side of the house demonstrates her signature mixed style particularly well. Here *Rosa* 'Ballerina' blooms under a boxwood topiary, pear trees are trained on the wall, and *Hydrangea macrophylla*, *Polystichum setiferum*, *Rodgersia aesculifolia*, and *Heuchera micrantha* 'Palace Purple' assure a long season of color and interest.

Over the years, Dina has written five practical books on topics such as romantic gardens; colorful, multiseason borders; dreamy plant combinations; and how she achieved magic in her own garden. "I have put my heart and soul into my garden," she says. "When I started, it was a new, special style not seen in Belgium before. Today it is a romantic garden full of colorful borders."

OPPOSITE A domed boxwood topiary accents a pink-themed planting.

A granite sett path surrounded by lush greenery leads through an oak woods
to a shady patio overlooking a meadow.

Vines are trained over the front door, and a pair of golden
yew domes anchor the plantings in the mixed border.

FROM TOP The naturalistic pond is an oasis tucked against a woodland and fringed in moisture-loving plants. • In the Courtyard, *Hosta* 'Crispula', *Geranium* 'Rozanne', *Rosa* 'Rhapsody in Blue', and *Delphinium* (Belladonna Group) 'Bellamosum' surround a pink astilbe in full bloom.

Garden Oostveld

OEDELEM, BEERNEM, WEST FLANDERS

EVERY YEAR, on the first weekend of October, Belgian landscape designer and plant breeder Chris Ghyselen stands at a rustic booth at the Great Dixter Plant Fair in East Sussex, England, quietly proclaiming the virtues of persicarias. He has been fascinated by the genus, with its bobbing flower spikes held above lance-shaped leaves, since he was a teenager. Today, as a plant breeder, his *Persicaria amplexicaulis* cultivars, including 'Black Adder', 'Fat Domino', and 'Pink Elephant'—to name a few—have become favorites of perennial enthusiasts throughout Europe.

In Belgium, Chris is also known for his garden design expertise, which is demonstrated to great effect at Garden Oostveld, which he started in 1990. Located in West Flanders about ten miles southwest of Bruges, the one-acre garden is long and narrow, rising thirteen feet from the front to the back. Around his property are flat, open fields, through which strong, incessant North Sea winds blow.

On the street where he and his wife, Anne Loones, live, hedges are *de rigueur*—but one particular hedge stands out from the rest. It is taller and more crisply shaped, with a thin slice removed through the middle—a minimal gesture that gives a hint of the design spirit at work in the garden within. Although hedges are commonly used in Flanders to create privacy and structure and to act as windbreaks, in Chris's hands, they delineate his garden's architecture, often with a playful, modern twist.

At the front of the couple's house, he has made a warren of intimate rectangular spaces with narrow paths. A sitting area is accented by topiary and hedges of various heights and shapes. Plants spill onto paving from small beds, window boxes, and pots. A padauk wood deck lines one side of a rectangular koi pond in a room of its own; on the other side is an untamed planting of rambunctious perennials that dip into the water as koi glide by. At one end of the pond, an elegant wooden Lutyens bench is tucked between topiaries and backed by a sheared hornbeam hedge.

Behind the house is the heart of the garden, a compact working area that includes the kitchen garden, a glasshouse, and a little nursery, where Chris breeds persicarias and sells plants. In the almost hidden, shady Stream Garden, a narrow path meanders alongside the water. The sounds of gentle waterfalls add to the atmosphere, along with a rich array of moisture-loving caltha, brunnera, carex, iris, veratrum, and ferny *Chaerophyllum hirsutum* 'Roseum'. It is easy to see why this is his favorite part of the garden in spring.

On the other side of the working area is an eye-catching, hundred-foot double border that Chris counts as is greatest success. Planted with late-season perennials and grasses in a boisterous naturalistic style, the borders are backed by loping wave hedges up to twenty feet high. Tall perennials are placed at the back of the borders, including white Joe Pye weed, *Vernonia arkansana* 'Mammuth', and *Helianthus* 'Carine', which can reach six feet. *Persicaria amplexicaulis* 'Firedance', *Vernonia crinita* 'Pure Purple', and *Sanguisorba canadensis* mingle with *Aster thompsonii*, *P. amplexicaulis* 'Fat Domino', and *Sedum spectabile* 'Joyce Henderson'. Being in this garden in late summer is "just like crossing the sea," he says.

Beyond the borders, Garden Oostveld becomes more and more naturalistic, with a Swimming Pond, Grass Garden, and Wildflower Meadow. There are no hedges in these areas, and one is likely to see cows looking over the fences. Chris has made sure that these spaces relate comfortably to the surrounding agricultural fields and the woodland, following one of his design principles: the farther you are from the house, the more you must look to the existing landscape for clues on how to proceed. "You also have to look back at your garden from the landscape," he says.

Naturalistic garden design is not common in Belgium, although interest is increasing. Once a year, Chris opens Garden Oostveld to the public, along with three other gardens he designed. The most frequent comment is something like this: "Very beautiful, but it must be a lot of work. How much help do you have?" The couple does most of the gardening themselves, with occasional help from a neighbor. "But," Chris muses, "I'm now in my late fifties. Maybe the hedges will be lower in the future."

OPPOSITE A stepping-stone path leads around the Swimming Pond surrounded by fresh spring growth, including *Carex elata* 'Aurea', *Iris pseudacorus* 'Variegata', *Chaerophyllum hirsutum* 'Roseum', and veratrum.

In September, the double border is still colorful, with *Persicaria amplexicaulis* 'Blackfield',
P. amplexicaulis 'Anne's Choice', *Symphyotrichum* 'Vasterival', and *Sanguisorba canadensis*,
along with cosmos, eupatorium, kalimeris, amsonia, and carex.

An elegant Lutyens bench overlooks the hedge-enclosed
koi pond.

FROM TOP The natural Swimming Pond is bordered by grasses and gunnera and a fruit-laden apple tree. • *Diphylleia cymosa* and ferns create a beautiful pairing on the boggy edges of the Stream Garden.

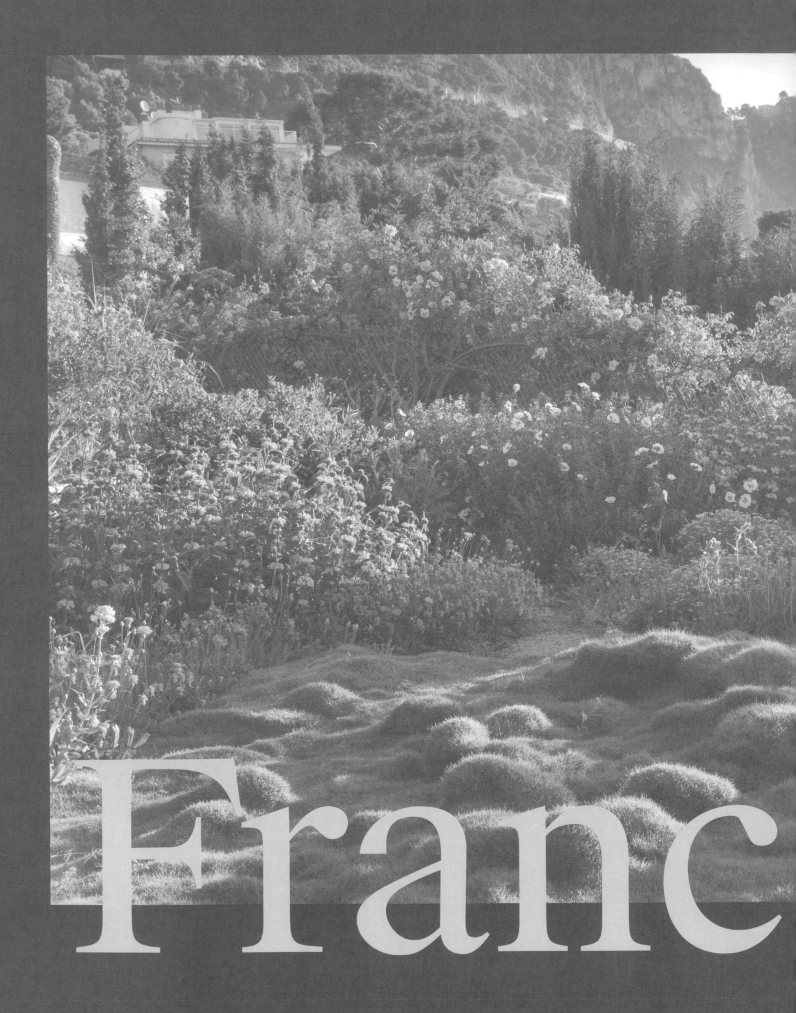

Franc

Château de Pange

PANGE, MOSELLE

BUILT IN 1720 for the first Marquis de Pange, on the site of a medieval fortress, Château de Pange is situated on the banks of the River Nied in the Lorraine region in northeastern France. The family has lived in the château since it was built, except during World War II, when much of its contents were looted. After the war, it became a children's home until 1983, after which the young Edith and Roland de Pange moved in and began refurbishing the estate.

By the year 2000, the de Panges were ready to address the outdoors. Working with the organization *Jardins sans Limites* (Gardens without Borders), a competition was launched to find a designer for the garden. They chose internationally renowned Louis Benech, because they admired the sensitivity of his proposed plan. "The spellbinding plant descriptions in his proposal made us dream," Edith said. Benech is best known for creating designs that respect the historical context of each site. He also includes a contemporary feeling with his plant choices and planting plans. This was a perfect combination for the couple.

Benech's plans for the garden began with the replacement of an asphalt parking area in front of the stately building with a more appropriate green entrance court. He created a broad, horseshoe-shaped lawn that follows the outline of an ancient moat that once protected the château. Boxy yew topiaries anchor the edges, and long wedges of *Miscanthus sinensis* 'Gracillimus' relax and soften the atmosphere.

On one side of the château, where neighboring buildings needed screening, Benech planted coast redwoods, giant sequoias, incense cedars, and a Concordia oak. A grand statue of Diana, the goddess of hunting, presides over the area, while nearby is an existing beech tree under which Edith likes to give poetry readings. As a final touch to this *petit parc*, Benech added groups of yellow-flowering *Koelreuteria paniculata* and sunny-leaved *Robinia pseudoacacia* 'Frisia'.

On the other side, where a stunning medieval barn angles away from the château, Benech made the Ornamental Gardens. Using the barn's colonnaded gallery as a starting point, he organized the space around a central axis, with a cruciform pool placed in the middle. Wide lawn paths extend from the pool in four directions, and large geometric swathes on either side are planted as meadows dotted with poppies, marguerites, viper's bugloss, and Queen Anne's lace that mingle freely with low grasses.

Two yew enclosures create rectangular spaces for more intimate gardens. One is planted in azure and silver to match the family's coat of arms. Mixed borders of *Perovskia atriplicifolia*, *Campanula lactiflora*, *Clematis integrifolia*, and white-flowered phlox and physostegia are enhanced by the silvery leaves of *Tanacetum macrophyllum*, *Anaphalis triplinervis*, and *Stachys byzantina*. The gracefully weeping branches of the elegant *Pyrus salicifolia* 'Pendula' shimmer with willowlike silver leaves.

The lawn outside the barn's gallery is higher than the rest of the garden and is sometimes used as a stage by the couple, who are amateur actors. Their outdoor performances of historical dramas welcome audiences of the entire extended neighborhood and other supporters of the château.

Opposite the green theatre at the far end of the Ornamental Gardens, Benech again turned to the château's history for inspiration. An eighteenth-century garden plan shows a butterfly-shaped enclosure there, and Benech used an approximation to make a holly-enclosed space for the impressive, classical statues of Pan and Flora, restored to their rightful places in the garden from before the war.

Throughout the garden are places that offer views of the countryside—the river, farm fields, rolling hills, and woodlands. It is a garden deeply rooted in place—"a garden in the country, and the country in the garden," says Roland.

The River Nied flows behind the eighteenth-century château.

The view across a meadow into the surrounding fields and woods exemplifies Roland's comment, "a garden in the country, and the country in the garden."

The statue of Flora, a nineteenth-century copy of a classical original, was
returned to a place of prominence in the garden.

ABOVE Benech planted *Miscanthus sinensis* 'Gracillimus' next to sober yew topiaries on the border of the lawn that replaced an asphalt parking area.

LEFT A block of meadow contrasts with the cruciform pool at the center of the Ornamental Gardens.

Jardin de la Louve

BONNIEUX, VAUCLUSE

NICOLE DE VÉSIAN began Jardin de la Louve when she was seventy years old. After she retired from working as a textile designer for Hermès, the high-fashion luxury goods manufacturer, she left Paris for the hilltop village of Bonnieux, determined to make a garden there. In her life before Bonnieux, she moved in the heady world of French style-makers and was known for her elegant taste, which she refined during the deprivations of World War II.

Located in the middle of Provence, the village is perched on a steep ridge with a church at the summit and earth-toned houses built along narrow cobbled streets with hairpin curves. At the bottom of the village is La Louve, which was named to honor the last she-wolf killed in the area in the last century. Nicole stumbled on the property while house-hunting for friends, and although it was a ruin at the time, she was intrigued by the bits and pieces of interesting stone she found in the overgrown garden. Without going inside the house, she decided to buy it.

As a young woman during the war, Nicole grew vegetables and fruit to feed her family. Much later, she made a different kind of garden for her Paris home and another that she could view from her office at Hermès. At a house on the French Riviera, which she purchased as a place to layover during work trips to Milan, she learned to prune back plants and cover the soil beneath them with beach rocks to help them survive without water between her infrequent visits. All of this experience she brought to Jardin de la Louve.

For ten years, Nicole created five terraces that flowed down her rocky hillside overlooking a valley. It has become her lasting legacy. The elements are simple. She clipped drought-resistant native evergreen plants such as boxwood, santolina, and rosemary into sculptural shapes and intuitively arranged them in asymmetrical, gray-and-green vignettes. Here and there, she inserted rustic accents of local stone, including balls, troughs, vessels, and stacked slabs crowned with irregular finials.

Her shaded Reception Terrace adjacent to the house is to this day considered one of the most masterful contemporary Provençal spaces in existence. The gravel terrace is intimate and inviting, simple and elegant, with informal places for sitting, where visitors are surrounded by Nicole's stone accoutrements and signature rounded and vertical topiaries, like beautifully assembled still lifes. On the lowest terrace, she created a tribute to the farm fields below the garden—repeated rows of lavender, each clipped into a mound, that erupts into purple flower spikes in late June.

The impact of this garden's style and ethos rippled through the Mediterranean gardening world. The modernity of her approach—using indigenous materials and plants, relying on the sculptural power of green architecture rather than flowers, working with the site instead of bending the land to her will, and the elegance of her pared down vision—continues to influence gardens far and wide.

When she turned eighty and wanted a garden on one level rather than on a steep hillside, Nicole sold the property to American art dealer Judith Pillsbury, who declared, "This is the most important work of art I own," and determined to maintain the original character when making changes or additions. During her tenure, Jardin de la Louve was classified by the French Ministry of Culture as a *Jardin remarquables* (remarkable garden).

In 2014, the property was sold to Sylvie and Pascal Verger-Lane, a couple from Normandy, who have followed the previous owner's lead and maintain the garden as a living work of art. "The strength of this garden," says Sylvie, after caring for the garden daily for the last five years, "lies in its sympathetic relationship to the land and in its extreme elegance."

OPPOSITE Nicole collected rough stone containers that revealed the marks of their makers.

A composition of clipped topiary in a variety of shapes and
sizes on a terrace as seen from the house.

Topiaries are assembled as artfully as objects in a still life.

In autumn, *Rhus typhina* offers a fiery display.

A stepping-stone path leads through low
grasses to a swimming pool.

The elegantly simple Reception Terrace is
filled with carefully chosen accoutrements
and topiary.

Jardin La Maison

MÉGRIT, CÔTES-D'ARMOR

LANDSCAPE ARCHITECT Clare Obéron has never drawn up an overall design for her garden near the village of Mégrit in Brittany. Instead, she says, "It has evolved as time and money have allowed, slowly. As a passionate plantsperson, I can never resist a gift or a new plant at a favorite nursery, and it has been the association and grouping of plants as an art form, an instinctive and creative process, where I am totally absorbed by having my hands in the earth."

After working as an architect in Paris, Clare decided to return to her first passion—working with plants—by starting Landscapes & Cie. In the country-side outside Mégrit, she and her husband were attracted to a tall, abandoned 1740 stone farmhouse on a two-and-a-half-acre plot. After they purchased the property in 1993, they began extensive renovation of the house.

As for a garden, there was nothing to speak of. The property consisted of a farmyard and some fields, with only three oak trees to the east of the house. "We began by seeding grass wherever pos-sible and slowly building up shelter from the strong winds with native hedging and some clipped beech," she recalls. "For several years, the main garden was the old yard to the front of the house, sunny and relatively protected. I remember planting here with a pickaxe to extract the stone whilst eight months pregnant with my second son."

Now, years later, with perseverance, patience, and optimism, the couple has changed nearly everything here. The house is restored, and a dairy barn perpendicular to the house has been converted into a home for Clare's mother. The garden today is a naturalistic and painterly refuge for her family and for wildlife. "Many plants have been and gone over time," she notes, "and as the garden has matured, favorite plants have been multiplied and repeated to create a sense of harmony and continuity through the different areas with accents of unusual specimens."

The house and the converted dairy barn, both faced in honey-toned stone, are situated perpendic-ular to each other and provide an attractive back-drop for the Gravel Garden. This bright, open space is a microclimate that nurtures less-hardy plants from the Mediterranean region, South Africa, and New Zealand. Clare added small islands or peninsulas that overflow with plants, with gravel paths flowing around them. Each bed is carefully arranged so that even in the dead of winter the garden is engaging. In the center, almost hidden by exuberant plantings, is a petite pond edged in thyme-draped granite and anchored by an exotic looking *Aralia elata*. Water dribbles from a tiny metal pipe arcing over a hollowed-out piece of thick granite, before slowly overflowing into the frog-friendly pond. The late Beth Chatto is one of Clare's horticulture heroes, and her influence can certainly be seen in this garden.

As one moves between the two buildings, the atmosphere changes. In the Gardener's Walk, a low dry stone retaining wall scribes a long, straight line and echoes the length of the converted dairy barn. Made from pieces of granite found on the property, the wall stages a deep tableau, where Clare plays with textures, colors, and shapes. The surface at the foot of the wall is covered in crunchy gravel. Slab steps cut through the wall and a short, S-curved path lead to a soft lawn—a transition to a new environment.

Clare has created sixteen named garden rooms in all, from a Four Seasons Garden, to a Thyme Garden, to a Fern Terrace. Now that most of the garden has matured, she is drawn more and more to the wilder areas in the back—the Meadow, Wild Garden, and Grass Garden—for the peace and tranquility she finds there.

"I feel that the garden sits comfortably in its environment, the scale of plantings complements the rather dominant house, and the 'exotiques' in the more sophisticated areas blend into the surrounding natural areas," she says, reflecting on her achieve-ment. "There is tremendous biodiversity and a natural ecosystem which continues to develop, perhaps the greatest reward."

OPPOSITE A vintage iron bench overlooks a colorful mixed border.

In the Gravel Garden, Clare included a diversity of plants to create her compositions.

Low-growing plants tumble over a stone wall, with a
resplendent *Viburnum plicatum* in flower.

FROM TOP Rustic wooden bollards surrounded by acanthus indicate a transition to a different garden room. • Amelanchiers dazzle when they flower in early spring.

Le Jardin Agapanthe

GRIGNEUSEVILLE, NORMANDY

LE JARDIN AGAPANTHE is a contemporary garden that is inward-looking creating a world within its boundaries altogether separate from the surrounding countryside. "The idea from the beginning," says Alexandre Thomas, the landscape architect and antique dealer who made the garden, "was to completely forget about what's happening outside when you are in the garden." With this garden, he hoped to make time stand still by designing an atmosphere that felt like a dream.

Alexandre was fifteen when he started the garden around his parents' home in the small Normandy farming village of Grigneuseville. He was beguiled by plants as a child and always said he wanted to be a gardener when adults asked. After training as a florist and then a landscape architect, he has created gardens for other people for the last twenty years. Le Jardin Agapanthe, however, has remained a place for personal expression and serves as a refuge from his demanding professional life.

Today his garden includes not only the original one-and-a-half-acre plot, but a second property across the street, which is less than an acre. Alexandre purchased the property in 2006 and installed the garden there a few years later.

Originally, the property was a flat piece of land, some of it a treeless cow pasture, which did not fit the vision in Alexandre's imagination. He started working with the elevations, digging valleys here and building knolls there. By the time he finished, the difference between the highest point in the garden and the lowest was about twenty-five feet. After he had moved all of this earth, the bare plot felt more spacious, the house seemed smaller, and the shape of the land called out for exploration, which was just the effect he had hoped to create.

He built a variety of steps, many meandering paths, small terraces, stone walls, and water features in every form, including streams, naturalistic ponds, fountains, and a formal lily pool. For his plantings, he focused particularly on lots and lots of trees, both evergreen and deciduous, because he wanted the landscape to feel like a forest. No part of the garden has a lawn.

Walking the myriad paths, each covered in pale sand that Alexandre adds to bring light into the garden, one can easily feel disoriented. "I love the way that it's like a maze," he says. "You can visit it in any way you want, and one of the most interesting things is the possibility that you will get lost." Along the paths, one brushes against hydrangeas, agapanthus, miscanthus, fatsias, and alliums, while overhead are bamboos, monkey puzzle trees, pines, weeping cedars, and palms. Topiaries shaped in balls, cones, and substantial spirals animate views. Vignettes set with vintage bistro tables, wire chairs, and antique terracotta pots give way to a long, metal arbor draped in wisteria. A stream with tunnel-like plantings is set with stepping stones leading to the light at the end. There is no discernable order.

In the center of the larger garden is a sunken area with a formal garden. An ornate double iron gate with stone piers forms the entryway to a rectangular space enclosed by a shoulder-height yew hedge. Along the perimeter are topiaries of varying heights and shapes, like a group of curious neighbors peering over the garden fence. Inside, four stone columns align with the gate piers and direct attention to a fearsome Bacchus mask fountain on the back hedge. On either side of a narrow central path, lavender is planted in a grid, the misty-gray mounds holding aloft dozens of purple-blue flower spikes. "It represents Italy, the sun, exoticism, and a total escape," explains Alexandre. "It's the most important open space in the garden, because here you can see the sun."

Alexandre calls the garden "the work of a lifetime," referring to how his preferences and the garden have changed over the years. His next project is to add lighting throughout the garden to generate a totally different perspective. In this new orchestration of atmosphere, he wants to open the garden at night to visitors. "They'll discover a garden completely different from the one they can visit during the day."

OPPOSITE An intimate vignette is created with a vintage bistro table topped with a bouquet of flowers gathered from the garden.

Sand-covered paths bring light into the garden.

ABOVE Wisteria blooms at the open gate leading into the garden.

LEFT The heart of the garden is an open, formal space that Alexandre designed as a tribute to Italy.

Stepping stones lead through a stream.

Le Jardin de Berchigranges

GRANGES-AUMONTZEY, VOSGES

IN AN ABANDONED GRANITE QUARRY in the Vosges, a range of low mountains in the Lorraine region of northeastern France, Monique and Thierry Dronet have created a singular garden. How the garden looks, feels, and functions results from each of their particular talents and interests, expressed in this unlikely place. "We both have a great sense of observation, are passionate, intense, creative, imaginative, and to a certain extent, pragmatic," says Monique, "and we are undeniably determined."

In the late 1970s, Thierry was "desperately looking for an unspoiled area" in which "to live in peace, and then I found these few acres of land in the Vosges." Over the years, he felled at least 1000 non-native spruce that were planted on the property during a government reforestation project in the 1960s, and he eventually brought in 1500 tons of soil by hand. "Until I met Monique years later, I expressed my creativity with whatever I found on site," he says. "I observed the way water was flowing down the hill to direct it into ponds and creeks. I assembled stones to form dry walls. I transplanted native plants here and there."

At the same time, Monique was becoming obsessed with plants. On a trip to England, she discovered cottage gardens, which were "so different from what I was used to in France, it enthralled me," she says. "I fell in love with the exuberant flower beds filled with perennials." On her next trip to England, she filled her car with flowering plants to take home and add to her garden.

When Monique and Thierry found each other, it was as if two pieces of a puzzle were reunited. "We completed each other so perfectly," explains Thierry, "her with that great knowledge of plants . . . and me with my need to express myself through nature." They started Le Jardin de Berchigranges in 1994 without any design principles in mind to guide them. "We did not plan it; we live it and it grows with us," he says.

Located at an altitude of 2100 feet in an area that receives almost 120 inches of rain each year, the garden is reached by following a winding mountain road through dark conifer forests. But when visitors arrive at the Welcome Cottage, the scene is decidedly expansive and the mood is cheerful. With a rippling, planted roof and hobbit-like doors, the low cobblestone cottage offers the first clue to the inventive spirits at work here.

The two main parts of the L-shaped garden are divided into a number of distinct, named areas. "Our garden is a story with many chapters or a symphony with numerous movements," Thierry remarks. "It is very green, has lots of curves, goes up and down and around, presents hidden rooms, an enchanting maze, openings in the tree canopy, shaded areas, babbling brooks and ponds, and so many views."

The first part stretches out from the azure blue house—Monique's favorite color. Impeccable lawn paths meander and flow over the undulating site and around crisp-edged perennial island beds, along ponds, streams, stone bridges, and rocks. Wood plank paths snake through lush plantings and sometimes end in spirals. The design feels organic, soft, and intimate.

In the longer part of the L shape, the named gardens are larger. Curves remain a dominant motif on the inside, but the spaces are blockier, with paths extending straight for some distance before joining in a large loop at the far end. Each space makes a big, confident statement: an impressive, mounded rockery opens to the sky; a playfully hedged, sloping space suggests that visitors imagine themselves descending as a pinball; and a fragrant garden inside a high-hedged octagon-shaped room is paved in an intricate parquet pattern that would be at home in any traditional house. On one side is a vast, bowl-shaped meadow that requires little maintenance—a quiet, sensuous space with a winding, grassy path rambling through large drifts of late-blooming perennials and grasses.

When asked what additions they plan to make in the future, Thierry replies, "We don't really plan the garden, but we intend to open a moss garden I've been working on for a while this year. You should ask Nature what she has in store for us in the long term. She inspires pretty much everything we do in the garden!"

OPPOSITE In the highest part of the garden, next to a swooping beech hedge, Monique has planted regal *Lilium superbum*, *Phlox paniculata* 'Blue Paradise', *Helenium* 'Moerheim Beauty', and echinacea.

The colorful flowers of the North American native *Allium cernuum* surround a mossy rock.

A path leads through the thriving kitchen garden, where a variety of vegetables are planted, including zucchini and mountain spinach (*Atriplex hortensis*).

The couple's azure-blue house overlooks the lower parts of the garden, where a rustic
fence demonstrates Thierry's construction style using materials supplied by nature.

FROM TOP A view of the upper garden from the road. • A boardwalk ends in a spiral sitting area built over a bog garden.

A wooden deck crosses a pond built by Thierry, backed by an exuberant
mixture of flowering plants designed by Monique.

Le Jardin Plume

AUZOUVILLE-SUR-RY, SEINE-MARITIME

IN NORMANDY, not far from Rouen, is Patrick and Sylvie Quibel's Le Jardin Plume (the Feather Garden), which successfully fuses the geometry of French formality with a naturalistic planting style verging on wildness. The Quibels' confident taste permeates every square foot of this original and artful scheme. "We had the advantage of having, on the one hand, a good knowledge of plants and also to have been interested for a long time in the design of gardens," says Patrick. The result is this sublime and inspiring place.

The five-acre garden, situated on flat agricultural land, surrounds a traditional Norman farmhouse and rustic outbuildings. The couple bought the property in 1996 and drew up a master plan within a few months. Their design was inspired by widely diverging styles, including the classical, seventeenth-century French gardens at Château de Vaux le Vicomte and the wild plantings at Henk Gerritsen's late-twentieth-century Priona Gardens in the Netherlands. Their garden would have a strong, rectilinear structure extending from the house, fashioned not by hardscapes but by plants—a kind of green architecture—contrasted with an exuberant planting style using mainly ornamental grasses and perennials. In 2002, the Quibels opened their garden to the public.

Visitors enter the garden on a brick path, walking between an early nineteenth-century restored barn and the sales nursery, which opens to a spacious gridded space called the Orchard—a Norman orchard reinterpreted in their own way. Wide, straight, mown grass paths, punctuated with native apple trees, demarcate squares and rectangles of native meadow grasses and occasional wildflowers. Each small meadow of about 110 square feet in size is repeated thirty-six times to the end of the garden, where a wire farm fence separates the garden from a pasture with grazing cows. The calming, rhythmic pattern is pressed against the level land and wide open to the sky.

At the top of the orchard, an austere, square pool is edged by mown grass. It echoes the little meadows in its proportions and simplicity, but with a dark surface that reflects the nearby apple trees and the cloud-filled sky. The Quibels consider this the heart of the garden, a sort of village green gathering place. Groups of chairs are placed here and there so that visitors can pause for rest and conversation. "I think we can say," remarks Sylvie, "that it is the large, square mirror pool and the apple orchard/meadow that are indeed the place that gives the garden a deep breath."

One step up from the Orchard and next to the house, the Summer Garden diverges from these spare designs. Here the Quibels have again employed a geometric grid, but this time it is used in a robust parterre that holds a sizzling array of perennials and annuals within a series of chest-high, crisply clipped boxwood rectangles. Inside each is a polyphony of gold, red, and orange flowers—crocosmias, sunflowers, yarrows, heleniums, zinnias, dahlias, and nasturtiums—that burst out of their boundaries in an ebullient display. The late-blooming Spanish flag vine (*Ipomoea lobata*) dances daintily in all three colors above the incandescent planting.

Not far away is Le Jardin Plume, the garden's namesake. The space is situated at an angle to the rest of the rectilinear garden, giving an opportunity to change the structural language. At the front is an arcing, hedged forecourt, and behind it stretches a magnificently playful wave hedge. A central path extends to a barn, and on either side are plantings light as air, with no broad-leaved plants or large flowers. Instead, the Quibels have planted tiny-flowered thalictrums and verbenas along with transparent sanguisorbas, delicate *Briza media*, and upright *Calamagrostis ×acutiflora* 'Karl Foerster'. The effect is atmospheric and effervescently fresh.

The garden also includes a Spring Garden, an Autumn Garden, a Miscanthus Basin, and a Potager filled with flowers instead of vegetables. Recently, they added a raised deck with a 360-degree view over the entire garden. Even in the bright summer months, it is easy to imagine the garden's patterns in winter, highlighted by heavy frost or fallen snow.

OPPOSITE In autumn, when apples in the Orchard are ripe, a dense miscanthus planting produces stunning masses of graceful buff-pink inflorescences.

The repetition of small-flowered perennials and grasses behind a stunning wave-cut hedge remind visitors of the garden's focus on the foamy flowers of these waves of plants.

ABOVE The wave hedge is perhaps the garden's most famous and most frequently photographed element.

LEFT An exhilarating mix of plants enlivens the Autumn Garden, including miscanthus, asters, and dark pink spikes of an annual persicaria.

La Jeg

LE BARROUX, VAUCLUSE

ON A SUNBAKED PROVENÇAL HILLSIDE is La Jeg, a garden with exceptional views across an agricultural valley to the majestic silhouette of Mont Ventoux, the Giant of Provence. For the garden's designer, Anthony Paul, who cares deeply about the way a garden sits in the landscape, the setting is perfect: "I sometimes feel that I fill in the foreground as on a stage while the background is done by a far greater hand."

Tony Stone, a London photographer and innovator in rights-managed photo collections, purchased rural La Jeg twenty years ago, seeking peace and quiet. He soon arranged for his friend Anthony, whose design practice is based in Surrey in southern England, to design a garden. Anthony's design had shaped the Hannah Peschar Sculpture Garden in Surrey, an enchanting outdoor gallery set in a woodland that exhibits contemporary sculpture, and Tony wanted his garden to include places for his own expanding sculpture collection.

By 2002, the bones of the design had been built, with the two-and-a-half-acre garden unfolding around the house and down the slope toward neighboring orchards and vineyards. Echoing the wider landscape, Anthony's design includes few straight lines and avoids grandness in the scale of the designed spaces. Narrow paths meander and rustic stone retaining walls hold back the soil, making comfortable terraces possible. Green nooks harbor sculptures as both surprising and honored focal points. The infinity pool, the most stunning feature in the garden, offers views of Mont Ventoux, and a small barn nearby has been converted to serve as a pool house. Artist Marzia Colonna's bronze figure *Man and Bird*, with arms stretched toward the sky, releasing a bird from one hand, is placed within a circle of water in one corner of the pool, an emblem of the garden opening wide to nature.

Visitors enter through a stone arch with a painted gray-green wooden gate and step down into a small, shaded courtyard. Vines drape over the courtyard walls, and informal paving zigzags across the space shared with a patch of lawn. A stepping-stone path leads through another gate to two terraces, the upper one an open lawn and the lower filled with waist-high, pillowy plants. Both are crisscrossed with stone paths that gently invite further exploration.

Straight ahead from the entry courtyard, the land falls off rapidly. A curving flight of stairs descends through repeated rows of rounded lavender that follow the curves of some imaginary contour lines. Below the infinity pool, the rows' direction reverses— a simple gesture that quietly turns the planting into a graphic design.

Provence, with sizzling hot summers and freezing cold winter winds, is not the most hospitable place to make a garden. "No sissy English garden plants will survive the rigors of a Provençal wind," says Anthony. Irises and cistus burst into bloom in late spring, along with statuesque *Ferula communis* 'Gigantea'. In addition to *Lavandula ×intermedia* 'Grosso', which begins its wonderful display in June and brings sound, scent, and mass color into the garden, he planted tough perovskia, santolina, and rosemary, with a color palette of lavender, chartreuse, yellow, green, and silver. In the lower orchard, wildflowers are encouraged to grow amid cherry and quince trees.

For many years, Tony has poured his creative energy into La Jeg, siting new sculptures and ensuring that his visitors have places to rest and reflect as they explore this special garden filled with fragrance and muted colors. In its maturity, it has become a haven for all creatures, where nightingales sing at dawn and dusk.

OPPOSITE The sculpture *Silent Columns* is by New Zealand sculptor Chris Booth. Phlomis blooms close by.

At dawn, Mount Ventoux comes into view over the infinity pool with the sculpture *Man and Bird* displayed in a shallow circle of water.

Row upon row of fragrant June-blooming *Lavandula ×intermedia*
'Grosso' echo the planting patterns in neighboring farm fields.

FROM LEFT Behind the house, where *Rosa banksiae* 'Lutea' clings to the wall, Anthony designed a fragrant garden, where two rills flow into a small round pool that connects to an eighteenth-century irrigation system. • Ceramic seats designed by English artist Hannah Bennet provide a place to relax in the lower garden.

Les Cyprès

VILLEFRANCHE-SUR-MER, ALPES-MARITIMES

BETWEEN THE BUSTLING CITY of Nice and the Principality of Monaco on the Mediterranean Sea is Villefranche-sur-Mer, a small town perched on the hills rising from a picture-perfect azure bay. With more than 300 days of sunshine each year and mild winters, this area attracts people looking for an active, outdoor life, which is exactly why Sandrine and Rudolf Schulz wanted to live here. After two years of searching, they found Les Cyprès, a half-acre estate with three houses sited at slightly different levels on a steep slope, each with spectacular views of the surrounding hills and sea and rugged limestone cliffs rising behind.

When the couple moved there, the gardens included the conventional Mediterranean elements— lawns, hedges, and palms. During the first winter, they decided to give these outdoor spaces a new life and sought out the help of garden designer James Basson. "We immediately liked his strong views on dry gardens," says Sandrine, "and how a garden should develop in the South of France."

James heads the Monaco-based firm Scape Design, an international practice he operates with his wife, Helen. Frequent participants in competitive garden shows around the world, their show gardens have won many awards, including Gold and Best of Show at the 2017 Chelsea Flower Show. The pair moved to the South of France from England in 2000, with a dream of making sustainable Mediterranean gardens. Their careful studies of plants in local conditions have led to their signature dry-garden planting style, which features locally sourced plants laid out randomly and chosen for their low water use and minimal maintenance requirements.

Construction of the Schulzes' garden began in 2011, and the gardens were finished a year later. The centerpiece for the main house is a sleek, new swimming pool that replaced an existing, problematic pool on the property. Several steps down from the house, the pool is on a broad terrace that hovers over the sloping terrain and is paved with Pierre de Bourgogne limestone, a quietly luxurious choice fitting the modern design. The water's surface here is like a mirror, playing with reflections of the sky and compounding the drama of the already splendid views to the sea. Six shapely multistemmed *Lagerstroemia indica* are installed in spare, built-in planters. One end is planted in *Zoysia tenuifolia*, a velvety lawn substitute.

On the other side of the pool, the land drops off rapidly. Dry stone retaining walls curve across the slope, creating planting terraces bisected by narrow steps. James and his team planted the area, as they did throughout Les Cyprès, with closely spaced, small plants that were watered once and never watered again. The idea was to cover the ground in the first year so that the young plants' roots would be shaded while they were establishing. Although the plants struggled the first two years, they were thriving by the third season.

The garden is planted with stalwarts of the Mediterranean Basin—lavender, rosemary, artemisia, and santolina. James and Helen added bright touches using *Phlomis* 'Edward Bowles', *Dianthus gratianopolitanus* 'Rotkäppchen', *Centranthus ruber*, and *Cistus ×picardianus*. This very natural looking planting contrasts and softens the hardscapes in the terraces and pools.

Sandrine and Rudolf are particularly pleased with the dry-climate planting at Les Cyprès, which reflects the textures and colors they would find on a walk in the countryside. "The garden fits so well in its environment that no visitor really believes that we created everything," says Sandrine. "It looks as if it has always been there. And this is a big success. Everything is in harmony."

A gravel path winds through the thriving plantings below the infinity pool.

OPPOSITE The garden was designed to be both drought-tolerant and low maintenance through careful selection of locally grown plants.

Within the planters in the sitting area around the Schulzes'
modern swimming pool is *Lagerstroemia indica*.

A beautifully crafted stone staircase leads
from the driveway to one of the houses on
the property.

Fine-textured *Zoysia tenuifolia* is used as a no-mow lawn.

Les Jardins d'Étretat

ÉTRETAT, SEINE-MARITIME

ON A HIGH, CHALKY CLIFF along the Alabaster Coast in Normandy is a new garden that feels as if, it could have existed in Alice's Wonderland. Russian landscape architect Alexandre Grivko created Les Jardins d'Étretat to please only himself after spending twenty years making gardens for others.

His property overlooks the charming seaside village of Étretat, an area visited by many artists and writers in the early twentieth century. When French actress Madame Thébault visited, she was so enchanted by the view from the top of the cliff that she purchased the sloping land, built a villa, and with her friend Claude Monet's encouragement, made a garden that included a vast collection of hardy orchids. Monet and other Impressionist painters were frequent guests at the villa and produced many paintings of the beach, cliffs, and the area's most famous landmark, a 230-foot natural stone arch and pointed rock formation called the Pinnacle L'Aiguille Creuse (hollow needle).

A century later, when Alexandre stayed in Étretat and learned that Madame Thébault's property was for sale, he knew that he wanted to make a garden there that would be open to the public. "I consider it to be my first personal creation," he says.

His concept for the garden was ambitious: He wanted Les Jardins d'Étretat to be an experimental garden laboratory and an open-air museum. He aspired to create a new garden style that drew inspiration from the patterns and shapes of the sea and cliffs, and that was based on neo-futuristic ideas—the belief in a better future achieved through the integration of art, technology, sustainability, and ethics.

He preserved the existing remnants of the historical garden, keeping the hundred-year-old trees and shrubs and restoring Madame Thébault's beloved hardy orchid collection. He also purchased some adjacent land, enlarging the property to about three-and-a-half acres. Construction began in 2015. By using the same methods André Le Nôtre had used at Versailles—employing a select but small number of plant species shaped into topiary—the garden was finished in two years and opened its gates to the public. In 2019, the garden received the European Garden Award for Best Restoration or Enhancement of a Park or Historic Garden.

Visitors enter the garden at the top of a steep slope. Below, the neat, half-timbered villa resembles a cottage in a children's storybook. Under lanky trees is an assemblage of clipped plants in every shade of green imaginable. Thickly clustered balls and domes of various robust heights arise from sinuous mats of clipped groundcovers; they seem almost animated, as though they had gathered for a welcoming reception.

On a steeper slope are row upon row of thigh-high, clipped plants that rise to the highest point, resembling a tea plantation. If one chooses to descend a zigzagging path, a large, white, translucent *Sea Shell* by Russian artist Alena Kogan floats into view. An oversized wind-up key jutting from a tree trunk plays music when turned; entitled *Clockwork Forest*, it was created by the British art collective Greyworld. Visitors soon realize that this is a new kind of garden—playful, imaginative, and filled with surprises.

Farther down the slope, the scene changes again. Set in the middle of several groups of low shrubs shaped like scalloped collars are bald, stout blue-gray heads with expressive faces: one smiles, another laughs, a third puckers its lips, and another sticks out its tongue. *Gouttes de pluie* (Raindrops), created by Spanish artist Samuel Salcedo, are engaging and surreal.

And so it goes in this garden, with one fantastical scene after another. Each of six atmospheric sections flows into another, showcasing Alexandre's ingenious sculptural topiary in a witty dialogue with the contemporary art he so loves.

In the lower garden, seven surreal, expressive head sculptures by Samuel Salcedo show a range of human emotions.

OPPOSITE Beyond spiraling hedges is a tribute to the property's history: a sculpture of Claude Monet, facing the ocean and the Pinnacle L'Aiguille Creuse.

For *Lounge Stones*, German object maker Thomas Rösler carved each
rounded form from a single piece of oak.

FROM TOP Alexandre designed a magical garden room furnished with Thomas Rösler's 32-foot-long *Table and Two Benches*, each piece made from a solid block of oak. • Terracotta sculptures, entitled *Until the Word is Gone*, by Russian artist Sergey Katran, hang from trees; each is shaped like the sound waves of the word "art" uttered in multiple languages, with accompanying audio.

The path leading to the house passes through the lower garden and the surreal heads created by Samuel Salcedo.

Spain

Ávila Jardín

ÁVILA, ÁVILA, CASTILE-LEÓN

OLIVE TREES are not typically grown in the northern regions of Spain, since they cannot tolerate freezing winter temperatures. Despite that, Gonzalo Lopez would not be swayed in his desire to include them in his garden. He called Urquijo-Kastner, a Madrid-based garden design studio, to draw up a plan for his weekend home on the windswept, rocky shores of a large reservoir. "His vision of the garden was one with clear references to the Provençal: olive trees, cypresses, lavenders," remembers Miguel Urquijo, who first met Gonzalo in 2014. "He was fixated on olive trees because his ancestors were related to the oil trade."

It took a second meeting and some research into the most cold-hardy Spanish olive trees for Miguel to agree to include them in the garden's design. "I must say we were both a bit frightened in the first winter," he recalls, but after three successive years of no olive deaths, they are now cautiously confident that the look Gonzalo wanted can be sustained.

The nearly three-acre garden is just a few miles north of Ávila, a picturesque provincial capital in the arid hill country northwest of Madrid, with a landscape that has more rocks than trees. Miguel and his partner and wife, Renata Kastner, made the most of the abundance of granite found on the property by using it to establish the garden's structure. A perimeter stone wall marks the boundary enclosing the whole property and defends the garden against wind and animals. Other walls define the cobbled arrival courtyard next to the house and the swimming pool area with its pergola and barbeque. Yet other walls retain soil to make functional level areas and to create terraces near immense outcrops to accommodate the soil needs for the olive trees. Each wall has been constructed in a traditional manner, with irregular stone and lots of little chinks in the joints.

By the time all the walls were finished in 2018—with a combined length of an astonishing 3300 feet—an important connection to the larger environment had been established. As Miguel says, "The eye travels easily from the garden to the landscape and back again."

Miguel and Renata then located olive trees that ranged in age from 70 to 500 years old. Sited generously throughout the garden, the trees quickly settled in, as olives of any age generally do. To contrast with the olives' shaggy, rounded heads, they included "the perfect dance partner," as Miguel puts it—the quintessential Mediterranean garden evergreen, columnar Italian cypress (*Cupressus sempervirens*). Together, these nearly obligatory companions established the atmosphere that Gonzalo wanted.

The garden also includes native stone pines, strawberry trees, and common hawthorns, which today provide important pockets of shade. Their varying heights enliven the garden's skyline and help soften the property's buildings and walls. Under the trees are mounding plants that lap over the edges of recovered granite cobblestones in the living areas close to the house and decomposed granite gravel paths farther away. Boxwood, lavenders, and shaped phillyreas and willows mix with caryopteris, euphorbias, salvias, ornamental oregano, and light-catching grasses.

Altogether, Ávila Jardín is an elegant, welcoming oasis in a rugged, sober landscape. "I'd like to think that this place represents a Mediterranean garden," reflects Miguel, "but with its continental component and strong character, it is probably more like the people and natural landscapes of this region."

OPPOSITE A decomposed granite path with craggy olive trees leads past planted borders, with *Nassella tenuissima* catching the afternoon light.

As one looks up at the many levels of the garden, the repetition of the planting scheme is evident, with Mexican feather grass, lavender, perovskia, and caryopteris nestled among the olive trees and Italian cypresses.

The garden's planting design is a combination of strongly erect verticals, low mounds, and loose grasses that move in the wind.

Stones collected from the property were used in the dry stone walls that enclose the arrival courtyard.

Finca Las Tenadas

COLMENAR VIEJO, MADRID

A SHORT DISTANCE north of Madrid, Finca Las Tenadas is home to an elegant, contemporary garden with plantings that are fresh and light as air. Enclosed on three sides by a renovated sheep barn, the garden completed the transformation of this property into an up-to-date event venue for celebrations of all kinds.

Owner Jaime Calderón asked gifted Spanish designer and plantsman Fernando Martos to design the three-quarter-acre garden with lots of open space—and it had to look good immediately. Fernando's plan was simple: twin rectangular gardens of slightly different sizes, united by a handsome iron Welcome Pavilion with breezy, wattle walls and roof covered in fragrant star jasmine and wisteria. "This is the heart of the garden," the designer says now.

Inspired by the design of Paley Park in New York City, Fernando planted a grid of *Gleditsia triacanthos* 'Skyline' in the center of each rectangle to provide soft, overlapping areas of shade. Long reflecting pools line one end of each of the gardens. "Water elements are always relevant to my gardens," he says. "I like the way they reflect plants and also the relaxing and refreshing sound they make." He laid buff-colored compacted gravel mixed with limestone dust throughout the garden—the perfect soft and natural surface for uniting the whole place.

Fernando cleverly lowered the grade at the centers of the gardens so that each planting bed slopes upward to enhance the views of its contents. Inside the deep beds edged with limestone—the material that also frames the barn's windows—is a refreshing plant mix. *Salix purpurea* 'Nana' pruned into refined gray domes contrasts with an alluring medley of naturalistic perennials and fine-textured grasses. *Panicum virgatum* 'Squaw' and *Nassella tenuissima* set a gossamer tone. Flower color comes from rugosa rose cultivars, Russian sage, daylilies, purple coneflowers, sedums, and agapanthus. The reseeders *Valeriana officinalis*, *Verbena bonariensis*, and verbascum fill gaps randomly in the complex planting for an even more natural look.

After years of patient experimenting with perennials and grasses, Fernando has compiled a list of plants that, with the help of drip irrigation, are not only resilient in the Spanish climate extremes, but display all the other qualities he wants for the gardens he designs. He was one of the first in his country to test whether it was possible for perennials common in England to survive the long periods of heat in his homeland. His interest in perennials formed after he worked as a gardener at Newby Hall in England, a country house known for having one of the longest herbaceous double borders in Europe. After three years there, he had fallen in love with perennials and grasses and was captivated by their naturalistic look, their changing character throughout the year, and their ability to move in a breeze.

The garden at Finca Las Tenadas epitomizes Fernando's ongoing effort to forge a new kind of planting style that fuses an alluring, loose naturalism with strong, structural elements. The atmosphere here is contemporary, artful, and breezy. Alfresco celebrations have never had it so good.

OPPOSITE Fernando placed several reflecting pools in the garden to mirror the sky and surrounding flowers.

The breezy Welcome Pavilion is the heart of the garden.

Beyond the vine-covered wattle walls of the Welcome Pavilion are trees planted in a spacious grid where tables are set for outdoor dining.

LEFT Fernando designed the garden to include an existing holm oak, which reigns over the garden.

LUR GARDEN

OIARTZUN, GIPUZKOA

IN THE BASQUE COUNTRY of northern Spain, a few miles from the French border near the town of Oiartzun, two landscape architects have been creating a garden adjacent to their studio since 2012, gradually expanding it to cover five acres. Iñigo Segurola and Juan Inarte, partners in the landscaping company LUR Paisajistak, use their garden to explore design concepts and test plant combinations.

Although most of the Basque region is characterized by steep slopes and narrow valleys, LUR GARDEN is situated on an alluvial terrace formed by the stream that runs along the perimeter of the site. "The flatness of the land was one of the key points that attracted and pushed us to begin the garden," says Juan. The garden's sixteen themed spaces, most partially hidden behind beech hedges, create a labyrinth of secret gardens.

Taking inspiration from the shape of an egg, Iñigo and Juan have used repeating ovoid geometry in the garden's large and small spaces, including clipped egg-shaped yews. This repetition of the form generates a coherent rhythm throughout the garden, in its separate parts and as a whole.

One enters the garden through a small woodland area, where large oaks grow between huge boulders along with tree ferns, Japanese maples, rhododendrons, and azaleas. Here the stream forms a natural pool, which Juan and Iñigo call a "gift from nature," because it required no intervention from them. Ahead, through the Red Garden, is the studio and greenhouse, a sleek one-story building with a flat, planted roof and floor-to-ceiling windows that face the garden.

In front of the studio is The Meadow, a broad, oval-shaped space with lawn paths mown around taller native grasses, making random, amoeba-like shapes that individually appear as casual doodles, but together create a cool graphic pattern. Within the meadow grass, they have planted flowers such as *Lythrum salicaria* and *Daucus carota* for color and texture in midsummer, when grasses begin to turn pale.

Nearby, an eighty-foot-long, egg-shaped pond of still water is the focus of the calm and tranquil Mirror Garden. Mown grass surrounds and grows up to the rim of the pond. Beyond the grass is the Yellow Border, planted in yellow, orange, and white perennials and shrubs. In August, with the explosion of flowering rudbeckias, this space reaches its maximum richness as the golden flowers are reflected on the water's surface.

Tetrapanax papyrifer is king in the Garden of Large Leaves. Juan and Iñigo indulge their affection for giant leaves with plantings of bananas, gunneras, rodgersias, and, most prominently, giant elephant ears. Round Corten steel waterlily containers are placed here and there, acting as foils to the Brobdingnagian scene.

Next to the stream, where it is most humid, is the shaded Jurassic Garden, with clusters of prehistoric horsetails and ferns. Adjoining that, in the darkest spot, is the small Moss Garden that was inspired by Japanese temple gardens. The partners created this garden after years of research on growing the diminutive plants. The White Garden and the Extravaganza Garden explore color themes.

Tall, bare tree trunks stand singly or in small clusters throughout the garden. They are remnants of decay-resistant *Robinia pseudoacacia* and are expected to last for thirty years. All are topped bluntly at about the same height, and together they have a totemic presence in the garden. "They're also a sort of joke," says Iñigo, smiling. "We call them the walking sticks of the goddess Mari from Basque mythology. She is the goddess of good and evil and the only deity the ancient Basque society had for thousands of years. In a way, we did this intervention to honor Mari, being completely sure that we would recover our faith in her. We think it is a very good way to start constructing a new world by paying homage to female behaviors that might lead us to a better society."

OPPOSITE The Meadow is in the center of the garden as a tribute to the original meadow that covered the entire plot. It consists of amoeba-shaped tall grass areas created by mowing short grass paths.

An elegant white-and-gray theme reigns in the White Garden,
where flowers and textures peak in July and August.

FROM TOP In the Mirror Garden, the pond's still, dark water perfectly reflects the flowers of the Yellow Border. • The blossoms in the Garden of Color Hydrangeas prove that hydrangeas can thrive on the Basque Coast.

Monfragüe Jardín

CÁCERES PROVINCE, EXTREMADURA

WHEN AMALIA AND CARLOS SORIANO bought a vacation property in the Extremadura region of Western Spain in 2007, they planned to live temporarily in a modified farm warehouse on the site until their house could be built. They asked design studio Urquijo-Kastner to create a garden on a relatively small budget, resulting in an uncomplicated design with a limited palette of plants. After all, it was temporary. More than a decade later, however, a new house has not been built. Instead, the temporary dwelling has been renovated into a comfortable home, and the garden, which has now reached a stable middle age, is permanent.

The Sorianos' property is located on an unnamed road in a remote, sparsely populated area, where the skies are big, the terrain is rugged, and the climate is harsh. Temperatures can climb to 110 degrees Fahrenheit in summer, and it is not unusual to go six months without rain. The immediate surrounding landscape is open pastureland with grasses, scrubby shrubs, and the occasional agave and prickly pear growing around holm oaks. Not too far away are the habitat-rich mountains of Monfragüe National Park, which form an arresting backdrop to daily life. When the Sorianos come to this place, they leave the urban life of Madrid far behind and step into another world.

As Carlos remembers it, he gave Urquijo-Kastner carte blanche, asking only that the garden require minimal maintenance and consume very little water. At that time, the area around the building was bare, except for a small olive grove at one side and a few holm oaks scattered about. Because the property was completely open to the vast pastureland around it, the designers suggested that as a first step, a rustic dry stone wall be built along the perimeter using stones found on the site. At four feet high, it would prevent animals from entering the property and define the half acre inside the walls as a garden.

For the planting, Miguel Urquijo picked up on something Carlos said in their first meeting: "He fancied the opuntia and agave plants growing in the area." They certainly fit the low-maintenance and drought-tolerant criteria, plus they were architectural in the extreme and full of personality. Miguel made them the key players in the plan and began calling them the king and queen of the garden. "Around them, everything subordinates and extols their majesties," he explains.

As for the rest of the planting, Miguel was influenced by a picture he had once seen of a simple garden with only agaves and ornamental grasses. "I had noticed the way the grasses softened the agave, and that was the starting point. If the client wanted agaves, I had to find a courtship of plants that would help to highlight their sculptural qualities but make sure they would also help to lower the aggressive points intrinsic in them." The perfect opposing companion, he decided, would be silky-soft *Nassella tenuissima* planted in light, billowy masses. Dotted about would also be perennials such as valerian, stachys, erysimum, dianthus, salvia, and lavender, and everywhere the soil would be covered with locally sourced gravel.

The resulting garden has no beds, no set paths, and, therefore, no fixed pattern. Instead, it evolves in accordance with each species' requirements—and reseeding whims. It is a garden in movement, where small pathways open between plants each year and other pathways close, although the king and queen always stand firm. "I would say," muses Miguel, "it is just a happy mix of plants that like to live and play together."

In the evening, the Sorianos relax on their large terrace, under a roof held aloft by beefy, reclaimed posts with a floor of salvaged granite slabs and cobbles. It is the perfect spot to enjoy the garden as well as the pastureland beyond. "I love that it moves," says Carlos. "It is a garden that is alive, very slowly displacing itself, changing its shape and form, showing different faces in different seasons."

OPPOSITE *Opuntia ficus-indica* thrive in the garden, here with fragrant *Pistacia lentiscus* and *Centranthus ruber* 'Albus'.

288

Agave americana and *Opuntia ficus-indica* are the dominant plants in the garden, along with perennials and shrubs including *Stachys byzantina*, *Euphorbia rigida*, and *Elaeagnus ×submacrophylla*.

MONFRAGÜE JARDÍN

FROM TOP A table and chairs under a holm oak are sited for dining with a view. • Because spiky agaves create a dramatic and threatening presence in the garden, the designers chose to surround them in soft, rounded plants. • A large, covered terrace shelters the family from the searing Extremadura sun and serves as a transition space between house and garden.

LEFT Cows graze in the pastureland just beyond the garden's wall.

Son Muda

FELANITX, MALLORCA

HÉLÈNE AND CHRISTIAN LINDGENS hadn't intended to buy a house when they traveled to Mallorca from their home in Zurich to play golf in the winter of 2005, let alone take on a rural ruin. But Christian became enamored with a dilapidated structure near the small town of Felanitx, with the idea of turning it into a vacation home. After the renovation of the house was finished, it fell to Hélène to figure out what to do with the nearly four acres of overgrown, scrubby land that surrounded it.

Like many of the neighboring farm fields, Son Muda is roughly rectangular in shape. And although much of Mallorca is hilly and mountainous, the land here is, as Hélène describes it, "flatter than flat." At the front of the property, the house stretches out crosswise, and behind the house is the majority of the garden.

Hélène had no experience with making gardens and knew even less about horticulture, but she began to educate herself by joining the Mediterranean Garden Society and visiting gardens and nurseries. She was particularly inspired by Heidi Gildemeister's garden, Torre d'Ariant, in the mountainous northwestern part of Mallorca, and Olivier Filippi's nursery in Mèze, France. Both are experts in dry Mediterranean gardening, and Hélène learned from them which plants could survive in Son Muda's hard, rocky soils without rain for five months in the summer.

Today, upon entering Son Muda, visitors are greeted by a boxwood parterre in the shape of a Tibetan endless knot, sited peacefully under the shade of tall trees. This is perhaps a prelude to the pattern-making and plant-shaping they will see elsewhere in the garden. Close by is the Morning Terrace, crowned by an airy loggia made of rusty steel and nearly enveloped in wisteria.

In back of the house, the scene is much more complex, cleanly linear, and unfussy. Using strong geometries—mainly rectangles—Hélène has laid out garden rooms in horizontal bands extending across the site parallel to the house.

In the Hedge Garden are repeated straight rows of a single species, some shaped as continuous flat-topped rectangles and others pruned into individual spheres. There is something vaguely agricultural about the planting here, or perhaps it is a deliberately modern interpretation of a classic parterre—a flat site that creates interest with a pattern on the ground plane. Either way, the garden is stylishly original.

Other rooms include the concentric-circled Celtic Cross garden, with each plant-filled ring displaying a different flowering or silver-leaved selection; the spare Mirror Garden, with twin aviaries at either end of a narrow reflecting pool flanked by variously sized ball-shaped plants; and the Pool Garden bordered by olive trees, with a sleek infinity pool and a stone pavilion. She has also created a gridded Olive Grove, a Herb Garden, a linear Labyrinth, a Forest, and more.

An early and inspired design decision was to use only white flowers in the garden, which Hélène believed would create a calm atmosphere. "I came from a hectic world. The theme of my life was chaos. I had a desire for peace and quiet, which moved me to make a white garden." She has now planted more than 1500 white roses in almost every room in her garden, with favorites being David Austin's floriferous 'Iceberg Climbing' and the highly fragrant floribunda 'Margaret Merril'. Along with the roses, she uses masses of *Gaura lindheimeri*, *Phlomis purpurea* 'Alba', *Erigeron karvinskianus*, and white forms of Dutch iris, hardy geranium, and salvia.

Making the garden at Son Muda has changed Hélène's life. She now has a design studio and builds gardens for others, employing forty-five workers. "In my new life and in my garden, I have learned more than in all the years before," she says. "Gardens are a school of life. I learned patience, tolerance, and humility. I learned to accept that not everything is in my hands, and I learned to live with fate, for nature will follow its own laws."

OPPOSITE At the front of the house is the Morning Terrace with a rusted steel loggia covered in white wisteria.

FROM TOP An overhead view of Son Muda shows Hélène's geometric garden rooms. • Tall trees shade the boxwood parterre in the shape of a Tibetan endless knot.

LEFT The narrow pool in the Mirror Garden is flanked by arrangements of sculpturally shaped plants leading the eye to an aviary.

The Celtic Cross garden is laid out in concentric circles of white-flowering and silver-leaved plants.

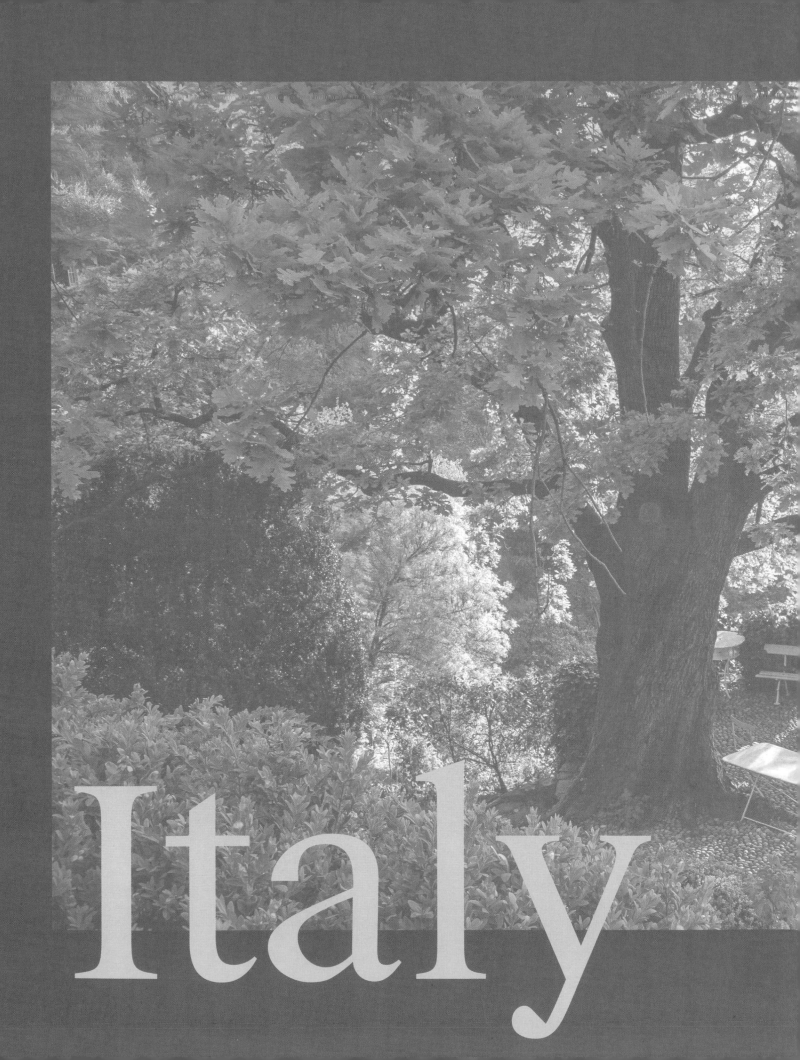

Italy

Bramafam

REVELLO, CUNEO

PAOLO PEJRONE is one of the most beloved and celebrated landscape architects working in Italy today. Trained as an architect, his young life took a sharp turn in 1970 when he met Russell Page, a prolific and accomplished English garden designer, who agreed to mentor him in the craft of making gardens. An internship in Brazil followed with modernist landscape architect Roberto Burle Marx. Since then, in his nearly fifty-year career, Pejrone has designed hundreds of public and private gardens throughout Europe and the Middle East. Despite all that, he has been known to say, "Don't call me an architect. I am above all a gardener" (Silvi 2019).

Bramafam is Pejrone's home, located in the hills above Revello, a small town in the Piedmont region of Northwest Italy. The house is sited in a steep corner of a valley and dates from the Middle Ages, with fortifications that were once used to protect the town below. His terraced garden of nearly thirteen acres is filled with so many luscious plants that the structure can barely be seen. "The garden develops freely and is what we call *esuberante* [exuberant]," he says. "I prefer to call it . . . a messy place, natural but full of life, where weeds can also be present, even if under control; ornamental plants are free to grow lushly and are only guided with small interventions. . . . I don't want a spic and span garden" (Silvi 2019).

More than anything else, Bramafam is a garden that shows Pejrone's love of trees and shrubs from around the world. Long before he came to live here in 1994, oaks and sweet chestnuts had been planted, along with cypress, phillyrea, arbutus, olive trees, and even *Phyllostachys edulis*—the world's largest hardy bamboo. To these, in the past twenty-five years, Pejrone has added plants as diverse as the Mexican succulent *Beschorneria yuccoides*, the lavender-flowered *Paulownia imperialis* from China, the Canadian hybrid *Cornus* 'Eddie's White Wonder', and the large-leaved *Magnolia tripetala* from the eastern United States. Each is planted in an appropriate microclimate produced by the hills and valleys on the property.

On a narrow terrace leading away from the house to the middle of the slope, a path makes its way through a cluster of rotund topiaries of varying heights to the vegetable garden. Pejrone has been growing edibles since he was four years old, when he was given his own little plot to grow radishes and salad greens. In this garden, the soil is rich from years of tilling with compost, and every inch is put to good use. Two large raised water basins, one placed above the other, provide water for the vegetables and give the eye a place to rest amid the intensely planted space.

Above the vegetable garden, Pejrone has created a small nook for comfort and rest on another terrace, in the dappled shade of the wide-spreading limbs of an old oak. Enclosed by casually clipped evergreens, white benches with faux bois arms and legs sit on pebbled paving just coarse enough to suggest an organic, nonrepeating pattern. Behind the alcove, lush *Hydrangea quercifolias*, camellias, and ferns cover the slope.

Farther away on another terraced slope is a grove of 700 olive trees that Pejrone says is Bramafam's biggest success. "They make a very good oil for the table and also they are the best-looking evergreens during the long winters." He has underplanted them with *Iris pallida* var. *dalmatica*, an old species iris, which makes the hillside an ethereal haze of lavender and silver in late spring.

For Pejrone, the garden he made in the deep valley at the bottom of the slope is the true heart of Bramafam, and this is perhaps an indication of how much affection he feels for his great magnolia collection planted there. Last year he added English hybrid *Magnolia* 'Caerhays Belle', and undoubtedly he will add more. Camellias, both sasanquas and japonicas, also thrive here amid flowering trees, hydrangeas, azaleas, and evergreen ferns. A pond is surrounded by bamboo and the striking, puckered leaves of *Gunnera manicata*.

May is Pejrone's favorite time in his garden, when the beguiling *Davidia involucrata* is in full bloom along with many roses, quince, peonies, lilacs, and any late-flowering magnolias. Altogether they make a grand landscape painting and represent the summation of a gardening life lived well.

OPPOSITE Large raised water basins not only supply water for the vegetable garden below, but also give the eye a calm place to rest.

Pejrone's colorful vegetable garden is on a
terrace with a view of his olive grove.

Pejrone has intentionally let his garden grow with an exuberance that allows plants to overtake the structure.

A fountain is surrounded by lushly growing plants, an example of Pejrone's relaxed attitude toward his garden's maintenance.

In the shade of an old oak planted long before he came to Bramafam,
Pejrone placed a table and benches in an evergreen-enclosed area.

A rhododendron blooms next to the emerging gunnera leaves and a flower spike.

Giardino Botanico di Villa Bricherasio

SALUZZO, CUNEO

IN NORTHWEST ITALY, in a valley in the foothills of the Cottian Alps, is a private botanical garden. Its designer and builder, retired farmer Domenico Montevecchi, single-handedly cares for Giardino Botanico di Villa Bricherasio. "My garden is a botanical madness, but it is also the source of my well-being. I'm happy when I look at a successful color or shape composition."

The garden is at the base of a hill near the town of Saluzzo that overlooks the Po Valley, a vast agricultural plain. The hill creates fortuitous microclimates in the garden that enable Domenico to grow a wide range of plants—more than 2000 species and varieties in all, totaling more than 36,000 plants from five continents.

Domenico's passion for the plant kingdom came easily. He was born with endless curiosity and a green thumb, he says. "I believe there was no beginning. I was always a gardener. My father and my uncle both had gardens. I grew up in them and learned. I always liked to sow seeds, to care for the seedlings, and to try grafting." As an adult, he became a kiwi farmer and worked in his garden in his spare time. Now that he has retired, he is happily able to dedicate himself completely to the garden.

The garden unfolds at the front of a dignified ochre-colored villa. Its three acres are carved into sinuous planting beds with a network of meandering paths, the intensity relieved by open lawns that become larger as one ventures away from the villa. Domenico has always been fascinated by mixed borders and draws on the memories of the many gardens he has visited on his travels to Great Britain. Nature itself has also been a source of inspiration. His close observations of natural habitats have helped him understand how plants with similar needs can be combined in conditions like dry soils, swamps, undergrowth, and alpine areas.

Close to the villa, the plantings are more intense, and this is where Domenico has placed his "elegant" plants—palms, sophoras, camellias, and maples—in sophisticated designs. Elsewhere, areas are devoted to a single genus, such as roses or hydrangeas, or to one plant type, such as bamboos or ferns. Still others are organized by habitats. Another plant grouping, unlike any of the others, is based on color—the "Only Blue" planting. Domenico's skill as a designer pulls it all together.

Perhaps the most stunning plants he grows are the tropical water lilies *Victoria cruziana* and *V.* 'Longwood Hybrid' in the largest of his ponds, and *Euryale ferox* in a smaller one. Aquatic plants have a special place in this plantsman's heart. He has surrounded the garden's ponds with gunnera, pennisetums, and panicums, which create exceptionally dramatic scenes.

When a group from the English Royal Horticultural Society came to visit Domenico and his garden, he was particularly pleased. The visit affirmed his lifelong passion, which he has expressed in this colorful, flower-filled, and exuberant place. When asked what his favorite time in the garden is, he replies, "May, at the end of the day. The plants and animals begin to rest, slow down, and I walk immersed in the perfumes and colors of my work." Then he quickly adds, "I hate winter."

A variegated dogwood lights up an area with berry-laden mahonia.

OPPOSITE A banana tree is a distinguished specimen, its beauty enhanced by the textures and colors of neighboring plants.

FROM TOP *Imperata cylindrica* 'Red Baron' is paired with buff-colored and golden grasses, each enhancing the colors of the others. • Domenico adds contrast in his plantings by juxtaposing large-leaved plants such as gunnera with small-leaved trees and fine-textured grasses.

LEFT One of Domenico's alluring color combinations in late spring includes lupine, aquilegia, and dianthus.

Giant Victoria water lilies are among Domenico's favorite plants.

La Pietra Rossa

SOLANAS, CAGLIARI

SARDINIAN DESIGNER Maurizio Usai was first attracted to English gardens, with their exuberant mixture of plants, as a teenager. He decided then, against all odds, that he would make that kind of garden at his home, La Pietra Rossa (the Red Stone), in the hot, red-granite-strewn coastal hills around Solanus, a village in Southern Sardinia. Contributing to his resolve was his instinctive rejection of the typical use of ornamental plants that he saw around him in the gardens of island vacation homes. He was offended by their "garish" colors and overuse of tropical flowers, in a "haphazard mix-up of plants without any harmony, where shapes and colors clash in unbearable chaos."

Maurizio honed his horticultural tastes during his childhood in the natural landscape near his home, which included native lavenders, almonds, euphorbias, and wild orchids. "It was made of intense colors that were not garish but had a clarity . . . that was never lost in our bright light," he remembers. "It had well-defined shapes and juxtaposed planes, a hierarchy of levels, moments of glory, and seasonal highlights."

He started his garden with roses, the quintessential English flower. He was fascinated by the fragrance and colors of English and old garden roses, but getting them to thrive in a hot, dry climate with gritty, poor soils was another story. "I was forced to adapt my wishes to the local circumstances, and I started then an endless sequence of adjustments," he explains. "I understood at once that I had to be ruthless and select only those plants that were able to give me the level of performance I was looking for."

More than twenty years later, Maurizio's relentless selection process has been rewarded, and he grows more than 260 different rose varieties in the garden. "In spite of the hard winds, the strong sun, the suffocating heat—apparently, in spite of every rule—they pay my constant efforts back," he says, with well-deserved satisfaction. "Nobody, when I started, would have guessed they could grow and flourish with such generosity and abundance."

Of course, being the plantsman he is, he grows other plants too. Many types of companion plants, from shrubs (including Mediterranean natives), to flowering perennials and annuals, to ornamental grasses, are combined in a style that some visitors have called "Anglo-Mediterranean." According to Maurizio, "Plants flow seamlessly into each other and I study their sequence with a careful eye for color and texture. The general effect I strive to achieve is that of an effortless, natural composition, that belies the careful horticultural techniques I keep refining, in order to achieve the best possible results in these peculiar growing conditions."

The garden has grown room-by-room over the years, from the original Rose Garden created prior to 1997, to a double mixed border added at the entrance in 2001. He planted a Hot Border a few years later, and then, in the hottest and driest area, he planted a sunken Mediterranean Garden.

Perhaps the most ambitious design is that of the Reflecting Pool opposite the main house. An old cypress hedge on the edge of the property was removed to reveal a splendid borrowed landscape of rugged scrub-filled hills. This gave Maurizio an opportunity to enrich the scene by siting the pool to bring the natural landscape into the garden. He added ornamental grasses, such as miscanthus, *Eragrostis trichodes*, *Melinis repens*, and *Pennisetum orientale*. South African and Australian plants are also part of this room, including *Grevillea* ×*semperflorens*, *Salvia lanceolata*, *Dietes grandiflora*, and *Astelia banksii*. *Rosa* 'Belle Portugaise' and the rare *R. chinensis* var. *spontanea* climb two majestic olive trees, and the blooms of *R.* 'Le Vésuve' are reflected on the water's surface. This airy composition, filled with harmonious colors and enlivening textures, offers a cooling oasis, designed by a very sure hand and eye.

OPPOSITE The sunken Mediterranean Garden features a blue-and-white color scheme, including *Centranthus ruber* 'Albus', *Rosa* 'Rival de Paestum', *Salvia* 'Indigo Spires', and *S. canariensis* f. *albiflora*.

Roses, foxgloves, and alstroemerias are
combined in a sumptuous display in spring.

FROM TOP Euphorbias and roses frame the view of a handsome terracotta urn. • Maurizio's romantic planting style emphasizes roses that tolerate the Sardinian summer heat.

The Reflecting Pool is surrounded by roses, grasses, and the lily *Dietes grandiflora* under a spreading olive tree.

LA PIETRA ROSSA

Gardens

ENGLAND

Broughton Grange
Banbury, Oxfordshire
http://broughtongrange.com

Bryan's Ground
Stapleton, Herefordshire
http://www.bryansground.co.uk

Cothay Manor and Gardens
Greenham, Somerset
https://www.cothaymanor.co.uk

Fairlight End
Pett, East Sussex
https://www.fairlightend.co.uk

Hanham Court Gardens
Hanham Abbots, South Gloucestershire
http://www.hanhamcourtgardens.co.uk

Hillside
Near Bath, Somerset
http://www.digdelve.com

Norney Wood
Shackleford, Surrey
https://www.norneywood.co.uk

Pettifers Garden
Lower Wardington, Oxfordshire
http://www.pettifers.com

The Barn
Serge Hill, Abbots Langley, Hertfordshire
http://www.tomstuartsmith.co.uk

Wildside
Buckland Monachorum, Devon
www.wileyatwildside.com

WALES

Dyffryn Fernant Garden
Fishguard, Pembrokeshire
http://www.dyffrynfernant.co.uk

Veddw
Devauden, Monmouthshire
https://veddw.com

IRELAND

Caher Bridge Garden
Formoyle West, Ballyvaughan, County
Clare
https://www.facebook.com/
CaherBridgeGarden

Hunting Brook Gardens
Lamb Hill, Blessington, County Wicklow
http://www.huntingbrook.com

June Blake's Garden
Tinode, Blessington, County Wicklow
http://www.juneblake.ie/cms

Sheilstown
Knockananna, County Wicklow
www.murphysheanon.ie

The Dillon Garden
Monkstown, County Dublin
http://dillongarden.com

SCOTLAND

Broadwoodside
Gifford, East Lothian
http://broadwoodside.co.uk

Hopetoun House Walled Garden
South Queensferry, West Lothian
https://www.hopetoun.co.uk

The Garden of Cosmic Speculation
Holywood, Dumfriesshire
https://gardenofcosmicspeculation.com

Whitburgh House Walled Garden
Pathhead, Midlothian
https://scotlandsgardens.org/
whitburgh-house-walled-garden

SCANDINAVIA

Marianne Folling's Garden
Rønnede, Zealand, Denmark
https://tidensstauderdesign.dk

Peter Korn's Garden
Landvetter, Västra Götaland, Sweden
http://eng.peterkornstradgard.se

GERMANY

Garten Moorriem
Elsfleth, Wesermarsch, Lower Saxony
https://garten-moorriem.de

HORTVS
Hilden, North Rhine-Westphalia
https://www.peter-janke-gartenkonzepte.de

Peter Berg's Garden
Sinzig-Westum, Ahrweiler,
Rhineland-Palatinate
http://gartenlandschaft.com

THE NETHERLANDS

De Terptuin
Mantgum, Friesland
http://www.nicokloppenborg.nl

Jakobstuin
Jistrum, Friesland
https://www.decoulisse.nl/jakobstuin

Lianne's Siergrassen
De Wilp, Groningen
http://www.siergras.nl/en/prairiegarden

The Stream Garden
Waspik, Noord-Brabant
https://vanmierlotuinen.nl

BELGIUM

Country Garden
Near Ypres, West Flanders
https://andymalengier.be

Dina Deferme's Garden
Hasselt, Limburg
http://www.deferme.be/index.php

Garden Oostveld
Oedelem, Beernem, West Flanders
https://www.chrisghyselen.be

FRANCE

Château de Pange
Pange, Moselle
http://www.chateaudepange.fr

Jardin de la Louve
Bonnieux, Vaucluse
http://www.lalouve.eu

Jardin La Maison
Mégrit, Côtes-d'Armor
http://www.landscapes-et-cic.com/
Accueil.html

Le Jardin Agapanthe
Grigneuseville, Normandy
http://www.jardin-agapanthe.fr

Le Jardin de Berchigranges
Granges-Aumontzey, Vosges
https://www.berchigranges.com

Le Jardin Plume
Auzouville-sur-Ry, Seine-Maritime
http://lejardinplume.com

La Jeg
Le Barroux, Vaucluse
tonystone.lajeg@gmail.com

Les Cyprès
Villefranche-sur-Mer, Alpes-Maritimes
https://www.scapedesign.com

Les Jardins d'Étretat
Étretat, Seine-Maritime
https://etretatgarden.fr

SPAIN

Ávila Jardín
Ávila, Ávila, Castile-León
http://urquijokastner.com

Finca Las Tenadas
Colmenar Viejo, Madrid
http://fernandomartos.com

LUR GARDEN
Oiartzun, Gipuzkoa
http://lurpaisajistak.com/v2

Monfragüe Jardín
Cáceres Province, Extremadura
http://urquijokastner.com

Son Muda
Felanitx, Mallorca
https://sonmuda.com

ITALY

Bramafam
Revello, Cuneo
archpejrone@libero.it

Giardino Botanico di Villa Bricherasio
Saluzzo, Cuneo
https://m.facebook.com/
giardinobotanicovillabricherasio

La Pietra Rossa
Solanas, Cagliari
https://www.lapietrarossastudio.com/
the-pietra-rossa-garden

Designers

ENGLAND

Broughton Grange and The Barn
Tom Stuart-Smith
http://www.tomstuartsmith.co.uk

Fairlight End
Ian Kitson Landscape Architecture &
Garden Design
http://iankitson.com

Hanham Court Gardens
I & J Bannerman Garden Designers &
Builders
http://www.bannermandesign.com

Hillside
Dan Pearson Studio
http://danpearsonstudio.com

Norney Wood
Acres Wild Landscape & Garden Design
https://www.acreswild.co.uk

IRELAND

Sheilstown
Murphy + Sheanon
http://www.murphysheanon.ie

SCANDINAVIA

Marianne Folling's Garden
Tidens Stauder Design
https://tidensstauderdesign.dk

Peter Korn's Garden
Klinta Tradgard
https://www.klintatradgard.se

GERMANY

HORTVS
Peter Janke Gartenkonzepte
https://www.peter-janke-gartenkonzepte.de

Peter Berg's Garden
GartenLandscaft Berg & Co.
https://gartenlandschaft.com

THE NETHERLANDS

De Terptuin
Nico Kloppenborg Tuinontwerper
https://www.nicokloppenborg.nl

Lianne's Siergrassen
Lianne's Siergrassen
http://www.siergras.nl

The Stream Garden
Van Mierlo Tuinen
https://vanmierlotuinen.nl

BELGIUM

Country Garden
Andy Malengier Tuin &
Landschapsarchitectuur
https://andymalengier.be

Dina Deferme's Garden
De Romantische Tuin van Dina Deferme
https://www.deferme.be

Garden Oostveld
Chris Ghyselen Tuinarchitect
https://www.chrisghyselen.be

FRANCE

Château de Pange
Louis Benech Paysaigiste
https://www.louisbenech.com

Jardin La Maison
Landscapes & Cie
http://www.landscapes-et-cie.com

Le Jardin Agapanthe
Alexandre Thomas Architecte Paysagiste
http://www.jardin-agapanthe.fr

La Jeg
Anthony Paul Landscape Design
http://www.anthonypaullandscapedesign.com

References

Les Cyprés
Scape Design
https://www.scapedesign.com

Les Jardins d'Étretat
Il Nature Landscape Design
https://ilnature.co.uk

SPAIN

Ávila Jardín and Monfragüe Jardín
Urquijo-Kastner Estudio de Paisajismo
http://urquijokastner.com

Finca Las Tenadas
Fernando Martos
http://fernandomartos.com

LUR GARDEN
LUR Paisajistak
http://lurpaisajistak.com/v2

Son Muda
Son Muda Gardens
https://sonmuda.com

ITALY

Bramafam
Studio di Architettura del Paesaggio
arch.pejrone@tiscali.it
archpejrone@libero.it

La Pietra Rossa
La Pietra Rossa Garden Design &
Landscape Architecture
https://www.lapietrarossastudio.com

Berg, Peter. 2018. *Nature. Aesthetics. Design*. Munich: Deutsche Verlags-Anstalt.

Donald, Caroline. 2011. Intelligent design. *The Sunday Times*, 1 May, https://www. thetimes.co.uk/article/intelligent-design-wct6bkgdq5q.

Grassino, Andrea. 2016. La natura si risveglia a Villa Bricherasio. *La Stampa*, 23 April, https://www.lastampa.it/cuneo/2016/04/23/news/la-natura-si-risveglia-a-villa-bricherasio-1.35017484.

Jencks, Charles. 2005. *The Garden of Cosmic Speculation*. London: Frances Lincoln.

Jones, Jody. 2015. Great plains: my prairie garden. *The Guardian*, 10 October, https://www.theguardian.com/lifeandstyle/2015/oct/10/gardens-great-plains-tom-stuart-smith.

Jones, Louisa. 2012. *Nicole de Vésian: Gardens, Modern Design in Provence*. Arles: Actes Sud.

Korn, Peter. 2008. Rock Gardening in Sand Beds. *The Trilium*, March–April, https://nargs.org/sites/default/files/chapter-newsletters/trillium-march-april-2008.pdf.

Mariasz, Ewa. 2010. "This is the Most Important Work of Art I Own – says Judith Pillsbury." *Ewa in the Garden*, 11 August, http://ewainthegarden.blogspot.com/2010/08/most-important-work-of-art-i-own-says.html.

Richardson, Tim. 2013. *The New English Garden*. London: Frances Lincoln.

Silvi. 2019. Il giardino Bramafam di Paolo Pejrone. *Le Cose Semplici*, 16 October, http://lecosesemplici.net/il-giardino-bramafam-di-paolo-pejrone/.

Stuart-Smith, Tom. 2014. *The Barn*. Vimeo video, https://vimeo.com/79310611.

Stuart-Smith, Tom and Sue. 2011. *The Barn Garden: Making a Place*. Abbots Langley, UK: Serge Hill Books.

Sunday Independent. 2017. 'Sell before you buy. Absolutely. I would have died of sleepless nights if we hadn't.' *Sunday Independent*, 26 March, https://www.independent.ie/life/home-garden/homes/sell-before-you-buy-absolutely-i-would-have-died-of-sleepless-nights-if-we-hadnt-35564486.html.

Wareham, Anne. 2011. *The Bad Tempered Gardener*. London: Frances Lincoln.

Wareham, Anne. 2017. Do me a big favour? *ThinkinGardens*, 22 December, https://thinkingardens.co.uk/articles/do-me-a-big-favour-by-anne-wareham/.

Wheeler, David. 2016. Bryan's Ground. *The Oldie*, April, https://www.theoldie.co.uk/article/gardening.

White, Maryanne. 2013. The Visions of Anthony Paul. *The Garden*, 17 January, http://agardenbydesign.blogspot.com/2013/01/the-visions-of-anthony-paul.html.

Wilson, Kendra. 2017. Bryan's Ground: Bloomsbury Revisited, on the edge of Wales. *Gardenista*, 10 August, https://www.gardenista.com/posts/garden-visit-bryans-ground-herefordshire-england-wales/.

Yurkewicz, Katie. 2010. Charles Jencks: The Garden of Cosmic Speculation. *Symmetry*, 1 October, https://www.symmetrymagazine.org/article/october-2010/gallery.

Photo Credits

Alamy Stock Photo /
   Sally Anderson, page 115
   foto-zone, pages 19 bottom, 34
   gardenpics, page 129
   RM Floral, pages 87, 88, 89, 90, 91, 94,
      95 top, 102, 103, 104, 105, 106, 107
   Steve Taylor ARPS, page 26

Iñigo Segurola Arregui, pages 285, 286, 287

Jurgen Becker, pages 152, 161, 162, 164, 165

Michael Burghaus, page 297 top

Ray Cox Photography, pages 108, 111, 112, 114,
   125, 126, 128, 130, 133, 134, 136, 137 top

DEA / W. BUSS / Getty Images, page 214

Marianne Folling, pages 141, 142, 143, 144

Dario Fusaro, pages 300, 303, 304, 305, 306,
   307, 308, 309, 310, 311, 312

GAP Photos /
   Matt Anker – Design: Tom Stuart-Smith,
      page 14 top
   Richard Bloom - Garden: Wildside Plants -
      Designer: Keith Wiley, pages 61, 64,
      65 bottom
   Mark Bolton, pages 32, 35
   Marcus Harpur, page 24
   Charles Hawes, page 251 top
   Charles Hawes - Veddw House Garden,
      Monmouthshire, Wales, pages 74, 75,
      76, 78, 79
   Jason Ingram, page 27
   Robert Mabic, pages 188, 189
   Caroline Mardon, page 22
   Jonathan Need, page 72 top and middle

Clive Nichols - Garden of Nicole de Vesian,
   La Louve, Provence, France, pages 222,
   224, 225, 226, 227
Clive Nichols - Pettifers Garden,
   Oxfordshire, page 53 bottom
Jo Whitworth, page 221

Ferdinand Graf Luckner, pages 166, 167, 168,
   170, 171, 270, 295, 296, 297 bottom, 298

Veronique Hostens, page 198 top

Robin Hutt, page 29

Peter Korn, pages 138, 147, 148, 149, 150

Gilles Le Scanff and Joëlle-Caroline Mayer /
   Biosphoto, pages 235, 236, 237 top

Robert Mabic, pages 172, 185, 186, 187, 201, 202,
   204, 205

MMGI / Marianne Majerus, pages 20, 23, 28, 30,
   43, 44, 46, 47, 55, 56, 58, 59, 62, 65 top, 80,
   92, 97, 98, 100, 101, 194, 212, 207, 208, 210,
   211, 241, 242, 243, 244, 245, 246, 258, 262

Andy Malengier, pages 197, 198 middle,
   198 bottom, 199

Fernando Martos, pages 279, 280, 282, 283

Noel van Mierlo, page 193 top

Huw Morgan, pages 8, 37, 38, 40, 41

Carolyn Mullet, pages 11, 12, 13, 14 bottom, 33,
   95 bottom, 137 bottom, 174, 175, 176, 178,
   179, 193 bottom, 237 bottom, 238, 264, 265,
   266, 268, 269

Clive Nichols, pages 15, 48, 49, 50, 52, 53 top,
   253, 254, 256, 257, 259, 260, 261

Claire Oberon, pages 229, 230, 232, 233

Caroline Piek – Garden Design: Van Mierlo
   Tuinen, pages 191, 192

Patrick Quibel, pages 249, 250, 251 bottom

Eric Sander, pages 215, 216, 218, 219

Claire Takacs, pages 17, 18, 19 top, 21, 66, 69,
   70, 72 bottom, 73, 117, 118, 120, 121, 122, 289,
   290, 292, 293

Miguel Urquijo, pages 273, 274, 275, 276

Maurizio Usai, pages 315, 316, 317, 318

Jaap de Vries, pages 181, 182, 183

Carl A. Wright, pages 83, 84, 85

Albrecht Ziburski, pages 155, 156, 157, 158

Index